THE BEAUTY of
the STORY

THE
BEAUTY *of*
the STORY

STORIES to TOUCH the JEWISH HEART

COLLECTED and EDITED BY ROSALLY SALTSMAN

The Beauty of the Story
   —Stories to touch the Jewish heart
© 2009 by Rosally Saltsman

ISBN: 978-1-60763-012-8

Editors: Rosally Saltsman, Roberta Chester
Proofreaders: Hadassa Goldsmith, Amy Lerner
Cover design: Rich Kim
Internal design and layout: Justine Elliott

THE JUDAICA PRESS, INC.
123 Ditmas Avenue / Brooklyn, NY 11218
718-972-6200 / 800-972-6201
info@judaicapress.com
www.judaicapress.com

Manufactured in the United States of America

ואולם בעבור זאת העמדתיך, בעבור הראתך
את כחי ולמען ספר שמי בכל הארץ.
(שמות ט:טז)

"However, for this I have let you endure,
in order to show you My strength and so
that My Name may be declared throughout
the world."

(SHEMOS 9:16)

ACKNOWLEDGMENTS

There are many forces and people at work in bringing a creative project together. Creation is an act performed alone only by Hashem. So it is to Him foremost that I must express gratitude for allowing me to work on this project and see it to fruition. I hope it inspires those who read it to draw closer to Him and serve Him with love.

My deepest thanks...

To Rabbi Paysach Krohn, whose stories I am privileged to hear firsthand. Rabbi Krohn is the undisputed master *maggid* of our time and he has taught me more than anyone else how incredibly powerful and life-altering a story can be.

To Rabbi Avraham Tzvi Schwartz, who keeps me technologically balanced and spiritually charged.

To Rabbi Yosef Wolicki, who taught me the power of rhetoric from the pulpit when I was a still a young girl, and the messages of whose stories still affect me today.

To Esther Susan Heller, the unofficial queen of the kingdom of Orthodox women writers. She sent messages to the far reaches of her kingdom to call forth stories from the wells of the hearts of the writers in her realm. To all those at Soferet, I thank you for answering my call.

To all the publishers who graciously allowed me to reprint stories that have appeared in their publications and who spread the word to their contributors in my name. I apologize if any attributions have been inadvertently omitted.

To the many talented and encouraging editors I work with, most notably Naomi Mauer of *The Jewish Press*, who motivates me from the other side of the world, and most especially Rebbetzin Sheindel Weinbach, who is a friend, mentor and spiritual "fairy godmother," always willing to encourage me and use her magic to rejuvenate my spirit or creativity.

To Sarah Shapiro, who is the Empress of the anthology. I have gained so much more appreciation for your work as story liaison in the Jewish world.

To Esther Sender, whom I have had the greatest pleasure in befriending and discovering a soul sister, and to whom I owe a debt of thanks for the title of this book.

To my son Joshua Israel Geller, *neiro ya'ir*, who found the quote for me at the beginning of this book, who lets me share all my stories with him and who is the star of the story of my life—till 120!

To all the wonderful writers who contributed to this incredible collection that spans the globe, the centuries and the tapestry of the Jewish people. I regret I couldn't include everyone who submitted a story, but I am extremely grateful to have read them all.

To Mr. Nachum Shapiro and Judaica Press, for taking a manuscript and producing a book, and to Roberta Chester, who is an editor's editor.

To all of you reading this, my sincerest and heartfelt gratitude, for a story is not a story without an audience.

May we always see the beauty in every story.

Dedication

To my son, who is my greatest inspiration—*ad mei'ah v'esrim!*

To my friends and colleagues, who generously gave of their time and talent to bring this book together.

To the readers, who provide the audience for the stories and whose Jewish hearts we reach out to.

To all those whose stories have yet to be told but are recorded in Heaven.

INTRODUCTION

The Jewish people are known as the People of the Book but they are also the People of the Story and we are blessed with many storytellers: the *maggidim*, the itinerant rabbis who went from town to town using stories to arouse *teshuvah* in the townspeople; the *cheder rebbi*s who used stories to introduce their young *tzaddikim* to the world of Torah; and parents who have been telling stories to their children for millennia to comfort and instruct them. Our whole tradition is encompassed by stories. Hashem commanded us to recount every year at the Pesach Seder the story of how we became a nation. And in addition to those stories that belong to all of us as our collective legacy, every one of us has many stories that are part of our individual and family history.

The stories in this book are just a sampling of the many stories of courage, kindness, faith and Divine Providence that fill our lives. All of the stories are true and have been verified as much as possible.

The most difficult part about putting this book together was choosing a category for each story. Any story that touches our heart reveals elements of Divine orchestration and miraculous events, highlights heroes and introduces us to Hashem's messengers as it underscores the fact that we belong to a nation apart.

I hope you enjoy these stories as much as I did.

Rosally Saltsman

CONTENTS

A NOTE ABOUT THE PRONUNCIATION
OF HEBREW AND YIDDISH WORDS

While most books standardize the pronunciation of Hebrew and Yiddish words, I decided that for the most part I would keep the stories in the original voice in which they were written. After all, the harmony of the Jewish people is created with everyone speaking, singing and telling stories in his or her own voice.

A glossary can be found at the end of the book with all pronunciations used in the book.

A NATION APART

The
DIPLOMA

BY YOSSI FAYBISH

*T*he year was 1959, in Botsami, a town in Romania. I was eleven years old, almost on the nose. Summer was rapidly taking its place of honor in the town. The blue and the green and the lilac's violet, the dominant colors in my life. My age was not worrying me, though, and certainly not the long summer vacation that was fast approaching. Rather, it was my mom's wrath once she discovered my bloodied figure I was dragging back home. I did everything possible to postpone the moment of reckoning by climbing a few more roofs and looking in awe down every tin drainpipe I could locate. Two of them had new nests in them, no eggs there yet but my joy at the sight overwhelmed any fear of things to come.

I hated it when the other kids and even some of the teachers called me *Jid*. I did not take any special pride in being Jewish, and I hated having my nose rubbed in it. Just like a kid, I readily adopted the communist idea of the absence of religion and equality for all, and as far as I was concerned, being Jewish in this small town, lost somewhere in the north of Romania, was just an accident. My history was Romania's history, and my heroes, the national poet born in my town and King Stefan, who once ruled the country. I knew the first one's poems by heart and the chapter on the second one in the history book by heart, too. I was a proud Romanian boy.

This time, as with all previous times, it happened with friends. We were playing "war" in the local public garden. My group was winning when someone got angry and called me *Jid*. In a few minutes, stones started flying and a few bleeding bodies scattered to their respective homes. One of them was mine. None of us cried, knowing that tomorrow morning we would all be as good friends as ever. For me, however, it was going home that was frightening. Finally, I had no choice but to drag my body home. It was getting dark, and if I wanted to get out again after dinner for another round of playing, I first had to get home.

My mom was busy in the kitchen, preparing dough for Saturday's sweet bread. I tried to sneak past her, but the dog started yapping happily and she turned around to see me. I stopped, seeing her look at me, and fixed my eyes on a rusted nail somewhere on the wall while the dog wagged its tail like it hadn't seen me in three days. I expected everything from "Your father will take care of you" to a serious spanking. Funny, not this time. I breathed with relief when she led me to a chair, took a towel, soaked it with water and then started cleaning the wound and wiping away the dried blood. She didn't even ask what had happened; it was not the first time that I had returned home bloodied from some street battle, but it was the first time that she seemed to take it easily, as if she didn't mind at all. She just gave me a new shirt and went back to her chores.

I was relieved. I knew my parents had been worried lately, and I wondered whether this was the reason I got off the hook so easily this time. They had filled in forms for immigrating to Israel, and my father was afraid it would cost him his job. There were fears of an unexpected knock on the door in the middle of the night. *Securitatea* (the secret police) was wearing them down. But none of this bothered me. The only worry I had was what would happen to our dog if we got permission to emigrate. The rest were grown-up worries. I ate my dinner and went out looking for my friends again, the hole in my head forgotten and new mischief on my mind. My mom just reminded me that next week the end of the school year's festivities would be taking place, and I'd better keep out of trouble or she'd find the stick she kept threatening me with.

For a moment, it flashed through my mind that this was the reason I had gotten off so easily; she was so proud of my grades that she just didn't feel like punishing me. It was just a flash of insight, and then I was off to the dark streets and another few hours of playing.

Monday arrived. I had finished fourth grade with exceptional marks. Fourth grade may not seem like much, so who cares? Well, I did, my parents did, and the whole town did. Food and clothing may have been scarce, but school was sacred and good end-of-year results, in any grade, were considered a national treasure and were celebrated with pomp and fanfare. I had been number one school-wide all my previous three years, and every year I looked forward to the ceremony, the handshakes and the diploma, three of which already hung above my bed. This was to be my fourth from this school. For my fifth year I would be moving to another school, a mixed boys and girls school, and I had wanted to finish this year once again as the school's number one student … which I did. My teacher informed my parents that according to my grades, they could expect to see my fourth diploma hanging next to the other three.

My father went to work as usual; he couldn't take the day off. But my mom was home and she was going to come with me, just like every previous year. That Sunday she arranged her hair with those hot round iron pincers that curled it. Then she bound the curls with colored small ribbons to fix them in place. On Monday she was dressed in her best clothes and best shoes. I was taking my bath for the second time that week, hating every moment of it but knowing it was a necessity. Then, I dressed in short blue trousers, a white crisp shirt, short white socks and new shoes bought just for the occasion (knowing they would give me blisters). The finishing touch was the freshly washed, freshly ironed blood-red pioneer necktie around my neck, the symbol of belonging, of excellence, and my pride and joy. We locked the door and went to the school. In her arms my mother carried a freshly bought bouquet of white gladiolas to offer the teachers when they called me up to the stage for my diploma.

We entered the big hall and looked around us, as always awed by the grandeur of the moment. The front row seats were taken by all the important party hotshots and a few guests from out of town. The rest of the rows were taken by kids and parents, family members and friends. On the stage was a long table with a green cover and about twenty chairs for the schoolteachers and some important guests who were supposed to deliver speeches for the occasion. At floor level, at the right side of the stage, a few upper-class pupils dressed in uniforms, had drums and trumpets and flags, ready to provide the fanfare. We decided not to sit down, but rather wait standing up somewhere at the back of the hall just to save me the embarrassment of having to crawl out between so many seated guests once I was called up. My mom greeted a few faces and was looking for my teacher when the ceremony started without her having found him. Even the kids knew that he had a drinking problem, yet it did not diminish any of his teaching skills. All the kids loved him, and I did, too.

Everyone rose for the national anthem. The drums beat the cadence; the trumpets called in triumph. I felt that the entire ceremony was for me and me only, once again the school's number one student. My mom stood proudly at my side, the flowers clamped tightly to her chest. Then everybody but the two of us sat down. The speeches started, but I never paid attention to all those long words and interminable sentences. I was impatient, waiting for my turn, embarrassed, yet one head higher than my usual size. My teacher was on the stage. He'd arrived late. We tried to catch his attention but didn't succeed. He looked a bit weary, kind of lost in a world of his own. Drunk again, I thought to myself, feeling a wave of love for the man who had been guiding me for four years now.

It was coming. The speeches were over, and a restless movement passed through the seated audience as the schoolmaster rose from his chair, the list in his hand, ready to start calling the names of the best students. Some heads turned around to look at us, knowing who would be called first. The drums again, then the trumpets. I started going forward without even waiting for my name to be called. I knew I was number one. A name was called. But it was not my name. I stopped, totally confused. A second name, a third. Not mine. Not mine. Kids were pushing through the rows of chairs, passing me on their way toward the stage, getting on it, shaking hands and getting handed pieces of cardboard paper. I was frozen in place. Tears started gathering in my eyes ... something was wrong, something was terribly wrong. The last name was called out. Not mine, either.

I felt a shape storm past me with unrestrained fury. I watched my mom's back rushing forward toward the front of the stage, stopping there for a moment and looking all those dignitaries accusingly in the face. Then, with one despising gesture, she threw the flowers to the floor. She turned around without a word, took my hand and pulled my tearful body out of the hall. At this moment, I fully realized for the first time in my life who I really was.

I was a *Jid.*

MY
JETBLUE *Minyan*

BY RABBI ZVI KONIKOV

I am on my way to Israel on El Al for a bar mitzvah of one of our Chabad members. It's 11:30 p.m. and, along with 450 other passengers, I am trying to get as comfortable as possible for the long flight to the Holy Land. My mind is reeling; I still can't believe what happened to me just a few hours ago.

I was regularly attending services daily, saying Kaddish in memory of my mother. JetBlue Flight 46 from Orlando to JFK en route to Israel presented a challenge.

The connecting flight schedules were very tight, so I arranged with my brother to take me from JFK to his Roslyn, New York, Chabad Center for afternoon services.

I had covered all possibilities … or so I thought. In Yiddish, there's an expression, "*Ah mentsch tracht un Gut lacht*—man proposes and Hashem disposes." This was a perfect example. We were supposed to depart Orlando at 4:15 p.m., but the captain announced a ninety-minute delay due to bad weather.

I had not missed saying one Kaddish since my mother passed away ten months ago. What to do? Worried, I thought of a solution. I'll exit the plane. I'll miss the flight. I can always rebook, but I can't miss Kaddish.

"Excuse me," I said to a stewardess. "I have an important meeting in New York, and if I can't make it in person, I must leave the plane now."

"I'm sorry," she replied politely. "We cannot return to the gate. We are on the runway waiting to take off. There are planes ahead and planes in back of us. We cannot move. It's impossible." Oh, well. I tried.

Thirty minutes passed, and we were going nowhere. Every few seconds, I looked at my watch and calculated our earliest possible arrival time. Another fifteen minutes passed. I realized I must do something, but what?

Suddenly, a crazy thought dawned on me. Maybe there were enough Jews on this flight to make a *minyan*. I didn't notice any religious Jews, but it was my only hope.

Before I make a scene, I'll check my chances of success, I told myself. Trying to be inconspicuous, I got up from my seat "to stretch" and walked up and down the aisles looking for Jewish faces. Alas, only the guy in the last seat had a Jewish face. And I wasn't even sure about him. Was I dreaming, or was I so desperate that I imagined that he looked Jewish? I gathered my courage and asked him straight out, "Are you Jewish?" I almost hit the roof when he answered, "Yes!" Quickly, I explained that I had to say Kaddish for my mother and needed a *minyan*. He understood. "Count me in when you get ten," he replied. Then he resumed his reclining position in front of the TV, nodding his head slightly to wish me good luck.

Bolstered by my success, I identified the next "Jewish face." Before I knew it, we were up to four. Each commented, "I'm not religious" or "I don't know how to pray." Still, they were willing to help.

The minutes continued to tick by, but I had run into a brick wall. That was it for Jewish faces. How many people who looked Puerto Rican could possibly be Jewish? Should I call it a day? Give up? Seat by seat I made my plea, but this time a little bit different than before. "Excuse me, is anyone in your party Jewish?" I asked. And the unbelievable was happening. Once in a while, the answer was "Yes, he is" or "Yes, I am."

By this time, I had seven. Only three more to go! Surprisingly, one of JetBlue's managers was sitting in a regular seat. "Can I help you?" he asked. I thought that he was just following the customer service routine. But when I explained my predicament, he immediately sprung into action to help me. I started to sing the JetBlue advertising jingle in my head. Amazingly, he offered to make an announcement asking for volunteers over the PA system.

"Thank you," I answered, "but I'm going to try to do this low profile."

"Excuse me," the man across from the aisle spoke up. "I overheard your conversation. I am Jewish." Now we had eight! I was beginning to believe it would happen. I continued my search. I began to get excited at the prospect of a miraculous *minyan*. But a bunch of people saying "sorry" and "no" brought me back to reality. One passenger who really wanted to help but wasn't Jewish said to me, "My buddy is half-Jewish." Hopefully, I asked his friend, "Are you Jewish?" "No. Not really," he answered. Disappointed, I turned to walk away. "But my grandmother was Jewish," he added. I turned and asked, "Your mother's mother?" "Yeah, but that doesn't make me Jewish, does it?" "You bet it does!" I told him. "Neat! Just like that, I find out I'm Jewish! Maybe the delay was worth it, just for that."

At "T minus one Yid and counting," I was roaring down the aisle with confidence now, ready to launch this nearly made *minyan*. By this time, no one on the plane had any doubts about what was happening. Every so often the manager would call out to me, "How many are we up to?" When I told him we were at nine, he radioed to the cockpit and asked if any of the crew was Jewish. "Negative," came the reply.

At this point, everyone wanted to help, but the situation seemed hopeless. I had already gone through every seat twice, and the dark reality seemed to be settling in that there were only nine male Jews over the age of thirteen on this plane.

As I was making my way back to my seat, crestfallen, someone who felt very sorry for me stopped me and said: "I have a Jewish friend in Georgia who I can call on a conference; will that work?" I explained why not and thanked him anyway.

I called my brother and told him the whole story. "You won't believe this: we've got nine people for this *minyan*! But that's really it," I said anxiously. "You're a chaplain in the sheriff's department. Maybe you can get a police escort to the plane, or maybe you can get someone Jewish from security to come out here and get onto the plane with us." He said he would try, but didn't sound too hopeful. Time and the odds were both working against us.

If I don't make this minyan *after getting nine Jews on this flight, what a letdown it will be*, I said to myself. Mentally, I was preparing myself for exactly that letdown because I had run out of options. I returned to my seat, just waiting to see what would happen next.

A few seconds passed before the passenger right behind me cleared his throat and confessed, "I'm really sorry, but earlier, when I told you I was not Jewish, I wasn't telling the truth. I was just very intimidated. I really am Jewish." My eyes became as wide as saucers. At first, I thought that he was pulling my leg. Either that or he was just trying to be nice because he saw how desperate I was. I was suspicious, and I knew I had to do a little questioning. "Is your mother Jewish?" I asked conversationally (as if I had all the time in the world).

"Absolutely," he responded. "Her maiden name is Horowitz. You can't get more Jewish than that." Then he added, "There's no question, I even know *Baruch Atah Ado–* ..."

Everyone around me became giddy with excitement. I signaled my loyal and devoted JetBlue manager, who was sitting about ten rows behind me. "It's a go!" I cried. "We've got ten!" You would have thought he had just won the lotto; that's how happy he was for me.

The manager invited me to meet with the stewardesses at the back of the plane. He wanted to make sure that the *minyan* would go smoothly. I went back and told them that there really wasn't much that I needed, and that I did not want to inconvenience them whatsoever. I suggested that they finish serving the beverages before we started so we wouldn't get in their way. Other than that, I told them that the afternoon prayer would take between seven and nine minutes altogether. I also thanked them for all their help and understanding.

The manager offered to let me know once they finished making their rounds through the plane. He would also help me gather my nine volunteers. As soon as I got the word from the manager, I started going down the aisles, "picking up" people. (I was hoping I'd remember who they were. I did.) It didn't take very long before a line of Jews was walking behind me toward the back. About three rows before the end of the plane, I noticed a face that I had missed. *He certainly looks Jewish*, I thought. With all these unknown people, maybe it's best to have eleven men, just in case. So I stopped and asked him, "Are you Jewish?"

He said, "Yes, but look, you're holding up the aisle! All these people want to get by!" I said, "These people are my *minyan*." Astonished, he quickly got into the spirit: "Well, then, I'm coming, too."

The atmosphere at the back of the plane was electric and ecstatic. The Jewish men were giving each other "high fives." We packed into the tiny galley kitchen in the back of the plane. The stewardesses barely had room to stand with us, so I politely suggested that they stand in front of us "to make sure no one disturbs the service." They happily obliged.

Before the *minyan* started, I briefed the non-religious members about what we were going to do. From their blank looks, it seemed as if only three of the eleven people had ever participated in a *minyan* before. While my main objective was to say Kaddish, I didn't want the experience for these secular Jews to be just lip service, so I decided to share a quick short thought on the concept of prayer.

"Prayer is not restricted to a particular place but can be done anywhere, from the privacy of your own room to a JetBlue plane that is stuck on the runway," I told them. Then I got to the nitty-gritty. "Since JetBlue does not, as yet, have ten prayer books for in-flight services, I will lead the service in Hebrew by heart. The only thing I ask is that you say '*Amen*' at the right time."

"How will we know when it's the right time if you're saying it in Hebrew?" one passenger asked logically. It was a good question. "I will give you the thumbs-up when it's time," I responded.

I took my yarmulke from under my hat and handed it to one of the men nearest me. The rest of the men made themselves at home in the kitchen and distributed yarmulkes (napkins) compliments of JetBlue. The scene was awesome.

A stewardess asked if she could take a picture of us in prayer, and I told her I had no problem with that at all. Without further delay, I launched our *minyan*. Outside, I felt like a million bucks when I gave my first thumbs-up! Inside, I was all choked up in gratitude to Hashem.

The *Amen*s were loud and emphatic. This bunch was definitely not shy or embarrassed of their heritage. The whole plane was buzzing. Napkin-covered men shouting *Amen* at each thumbs-up of this ancient-looking rabbi, as a stewardess snapped pictures. It was definitely not the typical scene in a JetBlue advertisement.

Despite the obvious humor of the situation, the men seemed quite touched, and stayed focused and serious throughout the prayers. I finished the prayers quickly and thanked everyone profusely for their time. Then we returned to our seats.

Almost immediately, the pilot announced that the hold was over. In minutes we would be departing for JFK. The feeling was incredible. It was almost as if the *minyan* was part of the schedule.

After the plane was in the air, one of the Jews from the *minyan* came over to my aisle seat. With tears in his eyes, he said, "I am totally uninvolved in Judaism, and I want to thank you deeply for this awesome reminder of my heritage!" Now it was my turn to be humbled. How one *mitzvah* leads to the next! What an unbelievable way to start my trip to the Holy Land!

IT'S
ALMOST *Shabbos*

BY ROSALLY SALTSMAN

*H*oward Margol was twenty-one years old in April 1945. He was a gunman with the 42nd Infantry Rainbow Division of the U.S. 7th Army, advancing through southern Germany. In the early morning hours of April 28, 1945, his unit moved into position near Dachau, a few kilometers north of Munich. Earlier that morning, Lt. Heinrich, the S.S. officer left in charge after his superiors had fled, surrendered Dachau to the Allied Forces. Margol didn't know anything about the camp, or concentration camps in general. But a smell reached him where his gun position was located. "It reminded me of when my mother used to burn the pinfeathers off the chickens before she'd cook them, the smell of the skin of the chicken being singed." A fellow soldier told him to come see the camp of over thirty thousand prisoners, the majority, Jews. He remembers the thirty railroad boxcars packed with the corpses of the Jews who didn't make it to Dachau alive.

In July, Margol was on occupation duty in Austria. "We were ordered to take a group of Jews who had come out of the camps to Hofgastein and Badgastein," Austrian resort towns where it was hoped they would begin to recover. In this idyllic resort, hot mineral water gushed out of the mountains and the elegance and refinement reflected no trace of the brutality that had created the barracks and crematoria of the camps.

The convoy of 150 army trucks, each carrying ten to twenty people, had been traveling all day. All of a sudden, throughout the convoy of trucks, the soldiers heard yelling and screaming. The drivers stopped to see what the problem was. The time was sunset, Friday afternoon.

The leaders of the group said, "It's almost Shabbos; we can't go on." Margol and the other soldiers who were Jewish said that they understood but that they'd be at their destination in twenty minutes, where warm beds and hot food was awaiting them.

"We can't go on. It's almost Shabbos."

The liberated prisoners left the trucks and sat down at the edge of the road. The army distributed blankets and tents, set up a field kitchen and prepared hot food for them. They remained there all Shabbos. After the sun went down the next day and the first stars were visible, they loaded up the trucks again to complete their twenty-minute journey.

"I had the feeling," Howard related, "that the main reason they wanted to keep Shabbos was that many of those Jews couldn't observe their Judaism the whole time they were in the camps, and now that they were free, they wanted to practice everything as best as they could."

In 1995, the fiftieth anniversary of the liberation of Dachau, Margol spoke of his experiences at a conference at Drew University in New Jersey. He told the story of the convoy held up for Shabbos. After hearing many speakers, the 3,500-member audience had begun growing restless, but at the end of his speech, they gave him a standing ovation.

Who knows how many of those people from the convoy are still living? But they made a *kiddush Hashem* of enormous proportions. They were no longer the victims of the barbaric Germany army. They weren't even taking orders from the American army. They were serving in Hashem's army.

Margol said, "It was a far greater emotional experience for me than Dachau itself."

CHESSED *without* BORDERS

BY RABBI CHAIM STEINMETZ

Shmuelly Beck* was a bright, inquisitive ten-year-old boy living in Brooklyn, New York. He enjoyed learning, playing and schmoozing with his friends. For all appearances, Shmuelly was a regular, happy fourth-grader.

Appearances notwithstanding, Shmuelly was different from his classmates. Very different. Shmuelly Beck had been born with renal failure due to complications at birth. Although his condition had stabilized by the time he reached one year, at the age of seven, he took a sudden turn for the worse.

Shmuelly lost his appetite and could only receive nutrition through a feeding tube. He began missing class frequently. Shmuelly's situation continued to deteriorate until his nephrologist informed his family of the grim news: Shmuelly would need a kidney transplant within the next four to six months in order to survive. Unfortunately, no family members were suitable matches for Shmuelly.

"It was like being hit with a ton of bricks," Mrs. Beck remembers. "In the back of our minds, we always knew it would probably happen, but now it suddenly became a harsh reality."

Miriam Oded, a young woman from the Bnei Brak area, had always been an idealistic and selfless person. She was also very reasonable and levelheaded, not given to impulsive decisions. Her family was at first taken aback when, at age twenty-three, she announced that she was interested in donating a kidney.

They initially reacted with surprise and some concern. However, after consulting with *rabbanim*, who gave their full consent and encouragement, the Odeds fully supported their daughter's decision.

Miriam Oded was not responding to a specific request. She had just done her research and discovered how safe and relatively simple it was to donate a kidney, so she wished to help a fellow Jew.

Following the Israeli government protocol, Miriam first took all the necessary medical and psychiatric tests and was determined to be an eligible donor. She was then evaluated by the government committee, who decided that a twenty-three-year old was not fit to make this decision. The evaluation team, unable to fathom the purely altruistic motives of Miriam Oded, concluded that she was either mentally unfit or unstable.

Miriam, however, was not so easily deterred. She continued her search to save others through different venues.

Eventually, Miriam Oded's selfless quest reached the offices of Renewal, an organization that provides comprehensive services to facilitate kidney transplants. As the director, I have seen my share of *ba'alei chessed*, but Miriam's determination to help others was extraordinary. Preliminary investigation indicated that Miriam would be an ideal match for Shmuelly Beck, the ten-year-old boy whom she had never even heard of. Shmuelly had been registered at a major medical center that had put him on their list to receive a cadaver kidney, a much less desirable option. Upon receiving the good news that a live donor was available, the Beck family excitedly called to inform the center of the good news.

How shocked they were to discover that the hospital maintained a strict policy of not performing transplants from unrelated donors. Unaccustomed to encountering such purely motivated *chessed*, they suspected an ulterior motive — such as a monetary incentive, which is illegal. Not missing a beat, Renewal arranged for the transplant to be performed at Montefiore Medical Center.

Miriam Oded was working with special needs children and did not want them to suffer from her leave of absence during the procedure. She switched jobs to pursue her goal of donation. Finally, the date was set for December 12, 2004, the last day of Chanukah. The Becks were still overwhelmed that a complete stranger from the other side of the world would so willingly do this ultimate *chessed*. With tears streaming down her face, Mrs. Beck kept repeating *"Mi k'amcha, Yisrael!* (Who is like Your nation, O Israel!)"

Only nine days later, too early a stage in Shmuelly's postoperative progress to hold a *seudas hoda'ah,* a grand celebration was held nonetheless. The event was important enough to prompt esteemed *rabbanim* such as the Matersdorfer Rav and Rav Strasser to attend.

In a certain sense, the *seudah* that was held at Avenue Plaza Hotel in Boro Park actually *was* a *seudas hoda'ah*. It was a *seudah* celebrating the nobility of spirit that was displayed by a remarkable young woman from Eretz Yisrael. It was a *seudah* giving thanks to Hakadosh Baruch Hu for imbuing His nation with this selflessness and the ability to rise to greatness. For in truth, all of us possess these deep reservoirs of *chessed*, but sometimes it takes an anonymous stranger, a distant cousin from a distant land, to remind us.

For more information about kidney donation, please contact the Renewal office at 718.431.9831.

All the names in this story have been changed.

A MATCH MADE
IN HEAVEN

SO WHAT IF
SHE'S OLDER *than Me?*

BY RABBI YAAKOV SALOMON

*T*hree weeks ago, I did something I have never ever done before. I danced at a cemetery.

It was a last-minute decision.

Mrs. Bernstein had been teaching for thirty years and had never attended a Torah Umesorah convention—a conclave designed to help inspire and instruct teachers in religious schools across the United States. But for some reason, this year her principal thought she should go.

So there she was that late May Shabbos afternoon in an audience with seven hundred other women listening to Rabbi Paysach Krohn, who had the audience riveted with his customary brew of drama, scholarship and wit.

"Everyone knows that there are thousands of wonderful, capable single men and women who are eager to get married," he thundered. "The problem is very complex, and so are the solutions. But one of the possible avenues to explore in helping to alleviate this very painful impasse is for men to consider marrying women who are older than them.

"There's really no reason in the world why men are so locked in to this idea that their wives must be younger. Widening your field of opportunities can make a big difference."

Most of the heads in the audience, Mrs. Bernstein's included, nodded in agreement. It did make sense. The notion that men needed to be older than their spouses seemed to be one of those ideas that just took on a life of their own, for no particular reason.

"As a matter of fact," continued the Rabbi, "one of the outstanding Torah personalities of the nineteenth century, Rabbi Samson Raphael Hirsch, not only married a woman who was three years older than he was, but also proclaimed the virtues and advantages of his unconventional choice.

"'I have many goals and aspirations in life,' he said at the time. 'I need a woman with a mature and responsible attitude who will help me fulfill those objectives. An older woman can do that.'"

Rabbi Hirsch was Chief Rabbi of Moravia in the mid-1800s and an influential member of the Austro-Hungarian Parliament before moving to Frankfurt. There, he was the rabbi of a community of just eleven families, which eventually grew to many thousands. His philosophical publications, *The Nineteen Letters* and *Horeb*, as well as his monumental commentaries on all of Torah, Prophets and Writings, have become staples in nearly every Torah home. This was a man whose every step in life was a lesson to generations that followed.

Those words were still reverberating in Mrs. Bernstein's mind the next day when Mrs. Gruman called. She knew of Mrs. Bernstein's son, Zev, and wanted to suggest a *shidduch* for him.

After extolling the virtues of this potential mate, Mrs. Gruman swallowed once or twice and confided, "I might as well tell you up front. The young woman is older than your son."

Zev was twenty-four and had only been dating less than a year. All the women he had dated had been younger, so why would he consider someone nearly two years older?

Yet the timing of this suggestion was too incredible to be ignored. It was just twenty-four hours ago that "for some reason" Mrs. Bernstein had heard a plea for men to consider women who are older and a story about a great Jewish leader who had done just that. Mrs. Bernstein tentatively continued to inquire about the young lady's personality and background.

"Tell me more about Esther," she said. "Tell me about her family."

"Well, her mother's maiden name is Hirsch. As a matter of fact, she happens to be a great-granddaughter of the famous Rabbi Samson Raphael Hirsch."

Mrs. Bernstein could hardly catch her breath. She probably looked around for the hidden camera, thinking someone was playing a prank on her. The coincidences were too unlikely to be mere chance.

After describing Esther to Zev and noting the rather remarkable signs that accompanied the whole process, Zev agreed to meet Esther.

I'll spare you the suspense. A few weeks later they were engaged.

Imagine the surprise when soon after, Rabbi Krohn received a call from Mrs. Bernstein, a woman he had never met or spoken with before.

"You don't know me," she told him, "but I owe you a great debt of gratitude."

She went on to relate in rapid-fire detail how she had never before attended this convention, had heard his unusual appeal, had received the call from Mrs. Gruman the next day, was told the Hirsch family connection, and now they were engaged.

"You're really the matchmaker here," she said.

This story does not end here. And I still owe you an explanation about how I came to dance at a cemetery.

For the past few years, Rabbi Krohn, a close friend of mine, has somehow found time to lead a nine-day summer tour of important Jewish locales in Europe. Every year, he begs me to join him to supplement his talks with brief lectures, musical accompaniment and camaraderie. "For some reason," this year I finally agreed. In August, a group of seventy Americans ventured to Germany, Prague, Austria and Hungary.

The trip was remarkable and included an itinerary that was spiritual, uplifting, pensive, mournful, picturesque and jam-packed.

On day two of the trip, we boarded our double-decker tour bus in Frankfurt. Next stop—the cemetery and gravesite of Rabbi Samson Raphael Hirsch. Thirty minutes later, we crowded around the hallowed and impressive monument of this legendary figure and listened as Rabbi Krohn described the accomplishments of this fearless, spirited and brilliant sage.

But what moved the crowd most was when he told the story of Zev and Esther, how they met and the role that Rabbi Hirsch somehow played in their holy union.

"I have no doubt that somehow ... somewhere ... this saintly man helped to orchestrate these highly improbable events," Rabbi Krohn said. "Don't ask me how, but this trip was organized many months ago—before Zev and Esther even met. How could he have also known that we would be here—at his very burial place—just hours after their wedding? Zev and Esther got married in New York last night!"

I felt a distinct chill travel up my spine. No one was unmoved; it was an inexplicable moment we would never forget. No one doubted that we were standing in a very holy place.

After visiting a few other graves, we quietly exited the imposing cemetery and made our way toward the waiting bus. But Rabbi Krohn had one final message for us.

"A cemetery is, of course, a very sad place," he said. "But how can we leave here, having experienced this extraordinary event, without dancing for the *chassan* and *kallah*?" Seconds later, guitar slung over my shoulder, on the sidewalk in front of this historic memorial ground, I strummed an A minor and led the group into a spirited celebration of wedding elation. None of us even knew the guests of honor, but it didn't matter. As if participating in the actual wedding, we joined hands and danced and sang like never before. It was an unforgettable scene of utter joy, unity and Divine Providence.

Several hours later, Rabbi Krohn called the new couple in New York—married all of one day—and told them what had just transpired. They were equally moved. Zev said that they would love to incorporate our dance into their wedding video.

Somewhere up in the heavens, I have a feeling that Rabbi Samson Raphael Hirsch was smiling.

And so was his wife.

THE DAYS
of LIFE *and*
LOVE

BY TOVA RHOEM

*I*took a deep breath and braced myself as I walked into the house and headed directly to the kitchen. The familiar room looked the same as always. The sparkling white counters were clean as ever, there was not one crumb on the floor and the dishes were all washed and put away. There was only one difference in the room, one change that had occurred in the woman sitting at the table. Savta was a woman who never sat. She was too busy cooking for the elderly, visiting sick people and taking care of her seventy-plus grandchildren to have time to sit. Yet now, she was sitting at the table as my grandfather stood mixing a small pot on the stove. He looked up when he heard my footsteps and smiled at me as he turned to my grandmother and said, "Ah, Tova's here. Maybe *now* you'll eat something." I chose not to notice the sharp tone of his voice.

I turned to my grandmother, who sat weakly in her chair. Her beautiful smile lit up her face, and she blew a kiss at me. "Tova, thank you so much for coming; I'm so happy to see you."

I smiled back at her and tried not to notice the black and blue marks on her hands, the wrinkles on her face, and the short little white hairs that fell from under her hat, all over her clothing. I chose to ignore the obvious physical signs of an elderly woman dying from cancer.

I smiled. "Hi, Savta. How are you feeling today?"

She waved her hand as if to wave away talk of her discomfort and said, "Never mind ... tell me what's doing with you. How was your date last week? And what happened with your job interview?"

I marveled at her presence of mind despite the difficult circumstances, the way that she remembered what was going on in my life, despite the fact that I am only one of her seventy-plus grandchildren. But before I could answer her questions, my grandfather's voice cut through. This time there was a pleading note in it, mixed in with the harsh command. "Tova, give her to eat. She needs to eat. I am leaving this bowl of oatmeal, and I expect it to be finished."

I smiled at him. "I'll try, Sabba." He walked out and went into the next room to do some learning. I turned to my grandmother, "Well, Savta, it looks like we're under strict orders to finish this."

She smiled weakly. "I wish I could," she whispered and then she made a gagging face. "I have no appetite; I physically cannot eat it, but it makes Sabba very nervous and upset. I don't mean to upset him." She was concerned for her *shalom bayis,* even in this state.

I slowly fed her a few bites, which she swallowed painfully. She was suffering from lymphoma, which affected her throat and made each swallow unbearably painful. After a few minutes, she pushed away the bowl and mouthed "enough." I didn't know what to do. I knew my grandfather would be back soon to see what she had eaten. He'd be very displeased to see a practically full bowl. I looked at my grandmother in an effort to try to figure out what to do. She pointed at the garbage can. Should I throw it out? *Could* I throw it out? I was literally scared to move. What would happen if my grandfather saw? He'd be furious at me! And was it the right thing to do? Didn't she need to eat to keep up her strength to fight the enemy inside? I looked from the bowl, to my grandmother's face, to the door and then, without thinking, I got up and quickly went over to the garbage, poured most of it out and ran back to my seat with the bowl. My heart was pounding, and I half expected my grandfather to come in the room to yell at me, and rightfully so. This was not a laughing matter; this was a matter of life and death. *Baruch Hashem*, my grandfather still hadn't come. I breathed an audible sigh of relief and looked back at my grandmother, as we both started laughing—me with my teenage giggle, and hers, a weak chuckle. Together we sat and laughed.

It felt like we were back in the past, in the days of her taking me shopping for Pesach dresses, teaching me how to make potato kugel and serving me chicken soup on Shabbos. We had gone back to the days of love, life and laughter where words like "lymphoma" and "chemotherapy" did not exist. My grandfather heard our laughter and walked into the room. He came over to the table, looked at the bowl and smiled, "See, I knew you'd be able to eat it. I guess being with Tova gives you an appetite." He looked at me, "I'm so relieved she ate; now I can go lie down a little."

I took a good look at him, the man I had been so scared of moments before. I looked at the worried lines on his face, the clouded eyes, the aching smile, and I saw a man who was suffering. True, he wasn't suffering from a physical disease, but he was suffering from the pain of his wife's illness and from the worry of losing her. I realized that his harshness wasn't anger and it wasn't cruelty. It was love, plain and simple—love for a wife of sixty years, who was slowly dying before his eyes. It was then that I realized that these days, the laughter may be hidden, but these are still the days of life and love, days of appreciating life and expressing love. He expressed his love by forcing her to eat;

I expressed my love by throwing out the oatmeal for her. I didn't know if I had done the right thing, but I knew that on that day, I had brought some relief to both of my grandparents in different ways. And I knew that the days of life and love had still not disappeared.

My grandmother was *nifteres* a month after this incident. *T'hei nishmasah tz'rurah bitzror hachaim* (May her soul be bound up in the bundle of eternal life).

COMING HOME

FROM ONE
SECOND *to the*
NEXT

BY NACHMAN SELTZER

*I*was young and sure of myself, I was handsome and smart, and I had it all figured out. Just because everyone else in my family was willing to undergo huge life changes didn't mean that I was ready to. It took some serious convincing, but Hashem had His way in the end (as He always does).

My family is originally from England. Our journey to Yiddishkeit is a fascinating story in itself, but I'm going to stick to just my part of the story. Suffice it to say, at the end of the day, my family had made an almost unanimous decision to move to the Holy Land. I say almost, because I hadn't voted yes, and wasn't in the slightest inclined to do so. I was happy for them, that they had found the light, but in my opinion, I couldn't see the end of the tunnel.

All of a sudden, though, after they had picked up and left, I decided to spend some time with them in Israel before beginning university, and what I thought of as "real life." From the start, although I wasn't willing to admit it, Israel impressed me a lot more than I thought it would. My parents were so anxious for me to see the truth, so hopeful that I'd come to the proper realizations, that I felt really bad letting them down. But I wasn't ready to give up my dreams.

The one concession I made was agreeing to take a Discovery Seminar. At this point, most people know what Discovery is all about. For those who don't, I can tell you that it's a veritable feast for the intellect. The professionals who run the programs can handle the entire gamut of crowds, ranging from open-minded people who have been *frum* their entire lives to the most hard-bitten, critical and sarcastic intellectuals imaginable. I fit into neither category and just made the most of the enlightening experience. I savored the proofs that they brought in abundance, the logic appealing to my brain and the proofs unassailable, however much the audience tried to shake the rabbi giving them. I marveled at the multitude of codes from the Torah and couldn't get over the message that every single thing in the entire world is clearly contained in its depths.

The final class is based on the Purim story, and the rabbi who gave it could have been an actor, with the kind of presence and charisma that had the class sitting on the edge of their seats while he played with their emotions. The comparison between the hanging of the ten sons of Haman and the hanging of the ten Nazis in Nuremberg was stunningly clear and scary, and the class got better and better until it reached its climactic ending, shocking one and all with the power of the message it presented. I was absolutely blown away! I told myself that this was the truth, that these people were right and that it was I who was close-minded and not the rabbis. And then I got on the next plane back to England and drove down to the university I'd be attending, located in the English countryside in a little city called Sheffield.

There are many cities in England, the land of the Greenest Hills. In London, Manchester, Birmingham, many of the country's citizens live in close, crowded confines, in neighborhoods of brick-covered homes, all attached to one another in row after row of pseudo-Victorian architecture, all conforming to the same specs. There are many buildings that are so old they have been designated as public property and need special permits to undergo renovation. There are also many neighborhoods in disrepair, which those who are on the dole call home. Not surprisingly, many people choose to live outside the cities in the little villages that dot the English countryside. These enchanted spots are spread out across the country. England has many inns where the same families have been living for hundreds of years with the most mysterious and curious names and trees, which have witnessed centuries come and go.

Sheffield, while not exactly a village, is not as large as the average city. It is a graceful place with the distinction of having played host to many of London's Jewish children during the German air force blitz in World War II. The city is a short distance from Manchester and many of the residents commute there to work. Having grown up my entire life in one of those densely populated cities, I found life in Sheffield a welcome change of atmosphere. The people were more relaxed and welcoming, there were parks, grass and trees everywhere, and I was surrounded by fellow students who accepted me as one of their own and even looked up to me as something of a leader.

I wish I could tell you that my conscience was bothering me, but that was really not the case. In the way of the world of today, I had no problem admitting that I knew the truth about something while just as easily deciding not to make it a part of my life. Besides, there was a whole new world to become part of. I was on the university campus, and to be honest I was a very popular member of the university. I had big plans for myself, and as far as business was concerned, I was going to go far in life. Living in Jerusalem really didn't fit in with those plans at all.

I got to know many of the other popular kids on campus, and we spent many hours involved in the favorite English pastime of "having a pint." Before, after and during classes, we could be found drinking together in any one of the numerous pubs in the area, and these hulking brutes became my closest mates. Once you share a couple of pints with the lads, the stories come out, and we became very close friends. The English pub is a world unto itself. With dark mahogany paneling and thick glass windows, it embraces the students in its steamy depths, allowing them to escape from the cold weather outside.

For the most part, I hit it off with everyone I met, save for one other guy named Dennis who felt that I was stuck up and a show-off. Since I desired to get along with everyone, I decided that I was going to win him over, and I accomplished this by humbling myself whenever I was around him. I felt that this was a small price to pay for the privilege of being his "mate."

Eventually his distrust waned, and we began to get along and became much closer. He introduced me to his group of friends, and since they were the most popular kids on campus, I felt like I had hit the jackpot. Here I was, barely eighteen years old and rubbing shoulders with kids older than me who had it all — money, fancy cars, you name it, they had it. And the funny thing was that they really liked me for who I was. They called me "Ely" and invited me to all their parties, and we traveled together and were there for one another; I felt like I had discovered the group of friends who would be with me through thick and thin. They would be my contacts in the business world and my network when it came to the job market, and I knew that I could rely on them, if ever I needed something they could help me with.

The year passed rapidly. Our friendship flourished, and anytime people asked me where the name "Ely" came from, I told them that my mother had named me after some old rock song that had been popular back when she was a teenager. Everyone liked that story, and the fact that I was Jewish, while not something that I consciously hid, was definitely not something that I advertised, either. It just seemed to me that the safest thing was not to bring it up. I fit right in with them, and there really was no reason for them to suspect that I wasn't just like them.

As the first year of university drew to a close, my group got together to discuss plans for the upcoming month of vacation. Some people would be touring Scotland, others had gotten jobs working for a nearby amusement park and others were going back home for a few weeks. The group I was closest with, however, was not interested in working and wasn't planning on any touring. Instead, we decided to stay right there on the university campus and just enjoy ourselves.

The semester came to a close. I watched the students leaving the dormitories. The parking lots emptied out, the study halls went utterly still. The entire university had disappeared. It was just my group of friends. We took advantage of the stillness. We played soccer and rugby and cricket and those guys drank more alcohol than I'd ever seen anyone drink before. It was vacation, after all, and they had no reason to stay sober.

Late one evening, I decided to go to a nearby store to pick up some groceries. Dennis accompanied me to the store, and as we were walking back to the dorm, the conversation turned personal in a way that made me uncomfortable. Dennis, you see, had smelled me out; something inside his brain, in the part that makes Jews different from non-Jews, had told him who I was.

"So, Ely," he drawled, "whereabouts are you from?" He was from Liverpool, and he spoke with the accent that is particular to that part of the country. I told him where I was from, and then he began grilling me about my family. Where had I grown up? How many children in the family? What did my Dad do for a living? The questions kept on coming, and I handled them as best I could, but then he began talking about religion. I could have told him anything I wanted. I could have said I was Lutheran or Catholic or Baptist or a member of one of the multitude of other religions on planet Earth. But I had never lied about being Jewish, and I didn't want to start then.

Besides, I had just attended the most amazing seminar about my heritage, and I knew that I'd never forgive myself if I lied about my very essence. So I told him the truth. I told him that I came from a Jewish family and that Ely was a Jewish name and that my parents and siblings were in fact right then living in Israel, and the atmosphere immediately cooled about one thousand percent. Then I requested him to keep the information I'd just told him secret, to which he agreed, and we made our way silently back to the dorm we shared at the university.

Needless to say, my dear "friend" Dennis didn't keep his word.

I walked into the common room, which was where we normally hung out, and was greeted with a silence so profound and disturbing that my hair stood on end. Where in the past I had been greeted by a chorus of "Hey, Ely," now the room was perfectly still. But my every movement was being followed by seven pairs of eyes staring at me in the most uncomfortable way. Please bear in mind that we were the sole inhabitants of the university. I could call out, I could yell for help, but there was nobody there who would be able to hear. For all practical purposes, I was alone in the desert, but at that point, I still didn't realize exactly what was going on.

I tried to act naturally, to start up a conversation, to ask the guys what had come over them, but deep inside my heart I knew what had happened. A voice inside yelled at me, "Be logical! These are your mates, your friends! They wouldn't dream of hurting you." My brain spoke to me of logic, but my heart told me otherwise. With the atmosphere changing so rapidly, I chose to follow the advice of my heart. I was attuned to my surroundings. Every sense in my body heightened with an intensity that meant that my body realized that it was in danger.

I could see "my friends" exchanging meaningful looks with each other, and I wondered what they had planned for my benefit. One of them went into the kitchen of the dorm we all shared and began mixing drinks for everyone there. Someone else switched on the CD player, and soon enough the guy in the kitchen came out with a platter of drinks. He handed them out and came over to me with the last remaining drink, which he offered me. They were all looking at me, so with no choice, I accepted the "kind" gesture and took the drink. I did not know what they had mixed into the drink, but I knew that whatever it was, there was no way I could allow myself to drink it.

Thankfully, the cup was made of thick plastic and was opaque, and when they all said cheers and proceeded to drink, I lifted my cup along with them and raised it to my mouth, acting as if I was drinking down a good gulp with them, convincing them that I was imbibing whatever vile brew they had put together for me, for the Jew in the dorm. I was sweating with fear, my Adam's apple bobbing up and down as I pretended to drink. I smelled the drink and it smelled funny. They looked at each other, and I think that they were waiting for whatever it was they had spiked my drink with to take effect. They were looking at me as if they were waiting for me to become woozy, to start falling off my feet, to begin losing control, and knowing that that was what they were expecting, I began doing just that.

I stumbled toward the door with a lurch in my gait designed to throw them off guard. They stared at me and laughed. I mumbled something about having to go to the bathroom, and they motioned me out with their hands. I left the room with its cloud of cigarette smoke and, straightening up, made my way to the bathroom where I emptied the still full cup into the toilet. My hands were shaking from fright, and my heart was beating at five times its normal speed. I couldn't believe what had just transpired in my very own dorm room. My friends had just tried to drug me! They were going to beat me up if I gave them half the chance. My friends! The people I wanted to spend my life with! I had to get out of there right away!

I left the bathroom quietly and made my way down the hall in the direction of the stairs leading to the next level. I would have taken the stairs to the ground floor, but the doors to the street were locked, it being the middle of the night, and I didn't have the keys on me. Suddenly, the door to my dorm room opened up and one of the guys came out. He looked at me with drunken suspicion, afraid that I was trying to escape, and asked me in belligerent tones where I was headed. I knew that I had to be tough with him. I walked straight into him, powerfully bumping into him and almost sending him reeling. I then told him contemptuously that I was going back into the room.

He watched as I headed in the direction of the alcove leading to the room. I turned into the alcove and he, satisfied that I was going back to my dorm, kept on walking to the bathroom. When I heard the door to the bathroom open and close, I quickly rushed out of the alcove and ran up the stairs leading to the next level. To get out of the building, I was going to have to walk right over my room, where they were all sitting. The ceiling was constructed from some paper-thin type of material that would allow anyone sitting underneath to hear the slightest movement, my footsteps included. But I had no choice; the alternative was too horrible to contemplate.

With infinite care, I began walking the tightrope across the floor, walking like an Indian, making as little noise as possible, praying the entire time that those people whom I had thought were my friends wouldn't hear my footsteps and come charging up the stairs to pull me back. Step by step, I almost crawled across the floor until I had reached the other side and could walk normally again. From the floorboards below came the sounds of a drunken party—wild laughter, the crash of broken glass and the sudden blast of music. I tiptoed over the remaining area and then broke into a run down the flight of stairs, which was unlocked and which led to freedom.

I left the dormitory with the clothes on my back and my wallet in my pocket. It was three o'clock in the morning, and I hailed a passing cab, telling him to drive me to Manchester. I must have appeared to be drunk. With my hair all over the place and my clothes dirty and disheveled, I probably smelled like a bad dream, but the cabby let me into his car, notwithstanding the terror reflected in my eyes, or perhaps because of it, and drove me away from Sheffield, away from my university and dorm and away from those who had been my friends, but who had changed sides the moment they found out who I really was. In the depths of my heart, I told myself that if they, the non-Jews, knew what it meant to be a Jew, then how on earth was I able to ignore it! Without meaning to, they had taught me one of the most important lessons of my life.

I stayed in Manchester for a week before taking a flight to Eretz Yisrael. As my plane taxied to a stop on the runway at Ben Gurion Airport, as the palm trees shook in the slight summer breeze and the yellow bus pulled up to transport us to the terminal, I knew that I had come home, that Hashem had stood by my side, and I hoped that He would continue to do so for the rest of my life.

This story was heard directly from Ely.

MY *Israeli*
TOUR GUIDE

BY PAMELA GOLDSTEIN

"**O**kay, look over there," said George, our Israeli tour guide. "From this one mountain we can see Lebanon to the left, Syria straight ahead, and the next peak over there is Iraq. Now, turn to your right … that's Jordan." He directed my daughter Miriam's attention back to Lebanon. "Two feet in front of you is where we were stationed during the Yom Kippur War. I was eighteen. We could see the enemy gathering on that mountain, right there, way more of them than there were of us …."

George continued to describe in great detail the battle that took place on Kafi Anan Mountain. His eyes were alight with passion, and he spoke so fiercely that we felt as if the battle were taking place again, right before our eyes.

My daughter's mouth was agape when he described how the Israeli soldiers set up noisemakers to sound like there were more of them on that mountain, and they prayed with all their might for the enemy to be deceived by the ploy. She heaved an enormous sigh of relief when George told us that the enemy became terrified by the noise and ran away.

So our tour went — day after day; no matter what part of Israel we went to, George told the history with passion and fervor, and with such incredibly minute and fascinating details that the place came alive. I could actually picture the chariot races at Caesarea's Hippodrome when George finished describing them.

"George," I said, "what is your education that you know so much?"

George laughed, feeling a little self-conscious. "An M.A. in history, a B.A. in religion, tour guiding courses."

"So why are you a tour guide?" I asked.

George smiled shyly and shrugged his shoulders.

We learned that George spoke eight different languages. Eight! Why would a man so obviously well educated choose to be a tour guide of all things? The question drove me mad.

George wasn't going to tell me why, either, so I watched him at work, trying to analyze him.

I began to notice little things, such as when we hiked in the Banias National Park, George carried a garbage bag and picked up any litter he passed. He fondly patted the walls at Megiddo and eagerly showed us the wild mustard growing there.

But it was when we were in an archeological site in Jerusalem that I finally figured it out.

"See this place?" asked George. "It's a *mikvah*, associated with King David's day. When I was fifteen, I spent my summer on this archeological dig right here, on this spot. I got here at six a.m. and worked so hard, sifting through the dirt, finding Roman glass and oil lamps. And do you know why?"

Miriam shook her head. George had her mesmerized, which was no small feat.

"Because at the end of the day," said George, "the head archeologist would come out and explain to me and the other kids the history of each artifact we had found. Tanach and history came alive for me. And the day we discovered part of David's palace wall? *Psheewww!* We celebrated for days."

George grinned. "No one has ever made as big an impression on my life as this archeologist. He showed me that the history in our Torah is still alive, here, in Israel, and we Israelis are living it. I couldn't get enough of it. I still can't. I never will."

I smiled at him. He had done exactly the same thing for my daughter. And there was the answer.

"And you love this place so much," I said, "that you want everyone who comes to Israel to see it and love it the way you do. You want us to realize how much a part of us is here, in this country."

George slowly smiled in acknowledgment at my discovering this truth. It was a fabulous smile. Bright white against his tanned skin, full of pride and *joie de vivre*.

"I wouldn't be able to do that in a classroom," he said.

"No, you wouldn't," I agreed.

"How many people have you escorted around Israel?" said Miriam.

"Thousands."

With any luck, I thought, he'll take thousands more around this lovely land—a land that, because of George, is forevermore in my heart.

# STONES

BY CHAVI CHAMISH

*T*he Jewish souls that pass through my life take my breath away. I touch a simple stone, and it is enough to conjure up for me the life of one individual whom I was destined to meet.

The year was 1990, and the great gates of the Soviet Union had opened. Jews flooded to Israel, the number quickly surpassing one million. May we be capable of comprehending this miracle we witnessed.

It was at this time that my husband and I responded to the call to volunteer with the arriving *olim*, and as a result, met the Tzoref family (Hebrew for "silversmith") who had arrived from Tashkent only the day before.

"What? It's not possible! You are telling me my name is a Hebrew name?" said Ilya to my husband, Pinchas. Pinchas had just placed a box filled with herrings, wine, cheeses, black bread and pickles on the kitchen bench, and Ilya's wife was looking at it, dumbfounded, her hands pressed to her cheeks, emotional and confused by this unfamiliar generosity of strangers.

Over coffee, we discussed many topics. What stays in my mind all these years later is Ilya, who bore the features of Jewish aristocracy, the high forehead, powerful Jewish profile and a *neshamah* that could dwell only in a Jew, telling us that his parents had not once made reference to religion. As a young boy, it had been his grandmother who had whispered to him not to believe what was written on the Memorial Stone at Babi Yar. "It was not 'over 100,000 loyal Soviet citizens' massacred in the ravine," she told me. "It was us, the Jews, whom the Nazis slaughtered—33,000 of our people were murdered in the first two days. I know, because I dragged myself from underneath the bodies. Never forget it. And never repeat it. Not even to your parents. The Communist Party forbids any reference to Jews at Babi Yar, and I am sorry to say, your parents would be very angry with me for telling you."

A few days later, the Tzorefs came with us to a Chanukah party in Ofra. As we drove through the ancient stone-covered Judean Hills, Ilya asked my husband if he would stop the car.

"I need to do something," he said.

With the sun beginning to set beyond the hills, Ilya lay face down on the rocky ground.

We stood a little distance away, sensing his need for solitude. Eventually, he sat up and said, "My grandmother was too ill to come with us on *aliyah*, though there is no other place in this world that she would rather be. Before we left, she called me to her bedside and said, 'Ilushka, it is said that when a Jew goes to Eretz Yisrael, it is as though he throws a stone from off his heart. Now you are returning our family line to Eretz Yisrael. I ask of you, please, when you get there, kiss the ground for me. It will be as though you are throwing a stone from off my heart, too. Always know that I am there with you.'"

Ilya looked around him and, with a sweeping movement of his hand, said, "It is as though these stone-covered hills are the physical proof of her words."

Years have passed since that trip to Ofra with Ilya, yet each time I drive through the Judean Hills, I recall that precious moment when Ilya cast off his stones. For me, it has become the symbol of our miracle, our triumph and Communism's failure to extinguish the precious Jewish flame.

THE
Old LADY

BY LEAH ABRAMOWITZ

his is the first Shabbat that there's no stream of neighbors coming to the old lady's house. No one drops by with hot soup, *burekas*, a thermos or potatoes cooked according to the Iraqi custom, the way she liked them.

As long as I can remember, as long as we've been in the neighborhood (that's thirty-four years), she was always old. She and her husband came to live in our courtyard about that time. We thought they were all alone. They lived like people once lived in the *maabarot* (transition camps) or in development towns. They cooked on a paraffin stove, heated the house with an old Friedman *neft* stove in the winter and lit the living room with a single 40-watt overhead bulb, so that the room was always dim. They had the barest furniture: an old table covered with a checkered linoleum tablecloth, a few rickety chairs, a cupboard that always had a door hanging on one hinge and a prevailing smell of Lysol.

After a while, it turned out that they weren't recent immigrants at all. He had, as a child, learned with the famous Ben Ish Chai in Baghdad, and had come on *aliyah* in the 1930s. She had given birth to nine children, but none of them ever came around. He was a tall, taciturn man, thin as a stick, whose nose was generally in a holy book. She ran the household as they once did in the 1940s. She would sweep with only the straw brush of a broom, bent over double, as she quite effectively cleaned the small apartment and courtyard. She cooked very little, and in the tiniest of pots. They were always known around here as "the *z'keinim*" (the old folks).

He died about fifteen years ago. Gradually, she, too, began to deteriorate. She became increasingly bent over, sickly and always alone. The neighbors in the next courtyard would bring her food; the boy who had miraculously survived a terrorist attack in India came regularly bearing goodies; my husband would bring in soup (even if we went away for Shabbat, he'd cook her his special chicken soup); and neighbors across the courtyard and from the third floor supplied hot water, casseroles and whatever else was missing. Most important, they came by to check how she was.

She generally spoke only Arabic (she'd never gone to school), but she was street-smart and very aware of what was going on around her. Even when she was sick, she'd make an effort to thank her visitors, quietly and with dignity. There was a certain nobility about her, even as she gradually grew older and weaker. Her children, at least those who we began to see, were another story. She had a divorced daughter who remarried and then was widowed very soon thereafter. Only when this daughter became homeless did she go to live with her mother, but never helped her or did things in the house. But when the old lady got sick, she disappeared altogether.

One of her sons was not 100 percent. If he was in the house when the neighbors brought her food, he'd grab whatever was brought in, swallow it quickly and sometimes yell at the neighbors. Mostly, though, he wasn't around very much. Her other children, who were reasonably "settled" (or their offspring), never seemed to take an interest in their mother's welfare. We couldn't understand it, but then we never knew what kind of relationship there had been, long before.

A week before she was hospitalized, the old lady took a turn for the worse. She became very weak and dehydrated. The neighbors met outside her door and discussed what should be done, whether to call the local doctor or get an ambulance. Taking an old person out of her natural environment, we all knew, was often fatal. Each one of us lovingly and patiently spooned water or soup down her throat for a day or two, but she hardly had the strength to swallow. The neighbors whispered among themselves that she wasn't young; rumor had it she was ninety-nine years old. Finally, it was decided to call the daughter who worked in a hospital as a nurse and have her make the decision. That was what eventually was done.

The old lady was taken to the hospital, where she was given liquid intravenously. She rallied and became her vibrant old self, but couldn't get off the bed. A few days later, we heard that she was transferred to a nursing home. "It's better that way," the neighbors said among themselves. "There, they'll look after her as she should be," they reassured each other. But really, each one of them missed the sweet, unpretentious old lady and the chance to help her, a mitzvah that had unexpectedly been snatched away from them.

Maybe there are other neighborhoods in Jerusalem where there are elderly people whom the neighbors look after. Maybe there are other neighbors who have adopted a lonely old person in their midst, who manage to provide not only nourishment and other basic needs, but also the attention and social contact every human being craves just as much. In our neighborhood, we don't have that right now. Our old lady is gone.

TRANSPORTED

IN
ONE HOUR

BY NACHMAN SELTZER

O ur taxi driver is as garrulous as they come. His name is Yacov, and he sure has a lot to say. He's a sweet guy and seems a little embarrassed by the fact that he drives a taxicab for a living. He has an opinion about every subject under the sun and is none too shy when it comes to expressing it. As we drive home from the Monkey Park, I can tell that he is driving carefully. He is just that kind of guy, the kind of person who makes sure to do everything in the right kind of way.

The road to Ramat Beit Shemesh is snarled in a mile-long traffic jam, and we crawl along, grateful that his air conditioner is in decent working order. It is as we pass the Shimshon Junction that he begins to reveal himself a little more.

"Look over there," he says to me, while pointing with his finger at the side of the road. "You see where I'm pointing?"

"Yes," I say.

"You see the bus stop over there?" he asks me, his brow furrowed, eyes narrowing as he stares out the window in concentration.

"Yes," I say again.

"Well," he continues, "every morning at five-thirty there are about forty soldiers waiting there for rides to different parts of the country. It's a busy bus stop." He pauses. "Of course, that also makes it a dangerous bus stop, since every terrorist knows that the best target is either a packed bus or a packed bus stop. Well, there I was at five-thirty in the morning—"

"Wait," I interject, "What were you doing there at five-thirty in the morning? Is that your normal bus stop that time of day?"

"Don't make me laugh," he says. "I never take the bus."

"So why where you there?" I ask him.

"I was on early morning patrol," he says, and I'm thinking, *Early morning patrol? What type of early morning patrol does a taxi driver do?*

"Yes, so there I was patrolling the area around the bus stop when I happen to notice that the ground about twenty feet away from the bus stop seems to be different than the rest of the area. It looks like it has been tampered with and my stomach gets this queasy feeling that says, 'Yacov, you better do something about this fast!' So I called the station."

"What station?" I ask him. "The taxi station?"

"No," he growls at me, "the police station, of course."

"I tell them what I saw, how the ground appears to have been disturbed and doesn't seem to match its surroundings. They get really concerned and send out another two patrol cars, and one of those vans that come equipped with enough equipment to defuse a nuclear bomb. By now it's starting to get lighter outside and the soldiers are beginning to notice the increase in police activity all around and they start getting nervous when I tell them to move away from the bus stop."

"They listened to you?" I ask him in surprise.

"Yes, of course. Why shouldn't they?" he says.

"Because you are a taxi driver telling them to get away, not a police officer," I say.

Finally he understands the source of my confusion. "That's the thing," he says. "I was a police officer, not a taxi driver."

Now I'm sitting there trying to understand what's going on. He was a police officer, a good one it seems. But now he's a taxi driver, so what exactly happened?

"Anyway," he goes on, "everyone moves away from the stop

and the van comes and they send in the robot and they discover that the ground was indeed funny and the reason was a twenty-kilo bomb hidden underneath the soil, poised to go off in a very short while. It was a miracle, plain and simple, that I caught it before it went off."

"Did you get an award?" I ask him.

"A citation of valor," he says. "Very nice. I had it framed and now it hangs in the living room."

Traffic is easing up by this time, and he presses down on the gas pedal as he squints from the glare of the sun. We drive without speaking for a while, and he scratches his head from time to time. His arms are sunburned and dark brown, and he sits in contemplative silence. As we pass the first entrance into Beit Shemesh, he begins to talk again, his words coming out quickly, tangling into one another like angry water rushing down a waterfall into the river.

"You know about the monastery?" he asks me.

"I've seen it from a distance," I reply.

"The monastery used to own all the land around Beit Shemesh," he tells me. "They have been here for many, many years and finally, when the price was right, they decided to sell. I don't know who designed their building, but whoever it was, knew a lot about architecture because it looks out over the entire countryside, providing the monks who live there with an amazing view of the countryside in every direction."

I shake my head in commiseration, knowing that something like this bothers every Jew. How can it be that in the land of our forefathers, we are subjected to the sight of a proud monastery overlooking our community, hovering over our heads like an eagle searching for prey!

"So that's the reason," says Yacov.

"The reason that what?" I reply, puzzled.

"The reason that I'm not a police officer anymore."

I don't understand, and I guess the look on my face confirms my confusion, so he says, "Okay, here goes. Listen well to the sad facts of life in the country of the Jews."

"About half a year ago, I'm sitting in the patrol car early one Monday morning when the radio begins to squawk and squeak. So I call the dispatcher and ask him what's going on, and he says that there's been a break-in at the monastery up on top of the hill. It seems that the monks spend much of their time creating works of art, which they sell to tourists, and much of their work had been stolen. So the dispatcher wanted to know which team was closest and available, to go see what happened and to take down the report.

"Well," he says, "as you can imagine, we were unhappy about this recent development, being that we were the closest team and the ones who were asked to go attend to the needs of the monks. Neither my partner nor I had ever been in a church in our lives, and neither of us was eager to see what it was like. But this was our job and we would just have to work something out.

"We drove up the long winding road to the monastery, which wound its way through some of the most picturesque scenery the area has to offer, still deciding who would be the lucky one to go inside.

"'Listen,' I told my partner Amram Cohen. 'I was never in a church in my life and I would really appreciate it if you went inside.'

"'Yacov,' he said to me, 'I was never in a church in my life, either, and I definitely don't want to start now when I'm old and gray.'

"We were at an impasse and were about to start arguing, something that we rarely did in the many years of our partnership, but just then we reached a crest in the road and the monastery was there before us, revealed in all its ancient, solitary strength. I knew that we had to make a decision now. We parked the car in the parking lot and stared at the ivy growing on the walls, neither one of us speaking, just waiting for the other to say something. Finally, I spoke.

"'You're sure that you can't go inside?' I asked him.

"'That's really the way I feel,' he replied. 'Besides,' he went on, 'I am a Cohen and as such should be on a higher level than the average man. I think it would be worse for me to go inside than for you.'

"To this I had no answer. I am no scholar and don't have much of a background in Jewish law, but what he was saying seemed to make sense. So it was settled; I was to be the *korban*. From the entire Beit Shemesh police force, I was the one who would have to go inside the monastery, something that I instinctively felt was wrong and which I had a powerful sense of foreboding about doing; as if only bad was going to come from this. But I had agreed to go inside and I couldn't really back out now.

"Amram stayed in the patrol car, while I got out and began walking to the official entrance way of the building, intending to get this over with as soon as possible. I remember that the flowers were in full bloom that day, shaking their little colorful heads at me as the wind whistled through the crisp air with a mournful sigh as if saying, 'Why yooooo, why yooooo?'

"I made my way over to the big wooden doors and was poised with my hand to knock, when the huge door opened up to reveal two monks standing in front of me.

"'Shalom,' I said, determined to be as polite as I knew how to be. 'I'm from the police department, here for the investigation.'

"'We know,' they said.

"*Oh, excuse me,* I'm thinking, *I didn't realize that you guys are such master mind readers.*

"I made a move to enter the monastery but found my way barred by the fatter of the two monks.

"'You can't come in from here,' he said, as I'm thinking, *Why not? This is the main entrance isn't it? What's up with these guys, anyway?!*

"'Follow me,' the fat one said, and I followed them silently around the colossal building until we arrived at the back. There, built into the stone wall, was a tiny door that reached halfway to my head. If I was going to have to enter the building from here, I would be bending down the entire time. *What a belittling way to have to get into a church!*

"But I was a guest at their place and I didn't want to get on their bad side, not after having received a five-minute schmooze from my superior about how we had to make a good impression. I merely looked at them in amazement, surprised beyond all words that they were making the police officer who had arrived to assist them do something so demeaning. Then I pulled opened the diminutive door and bent down and then down some more until I was able to see where I was going. I wanted to make sure that I had a clear view just in case there were some steep stairs leading to the dungeons or something, and then when I fell down the stairs, they would say, 'Well, what do you want? The man wasn't looking where he was going.'

"Instead of seeing a hallway like I thought I would, I saw two gigantic statues standing in front of me, and in that split second I realized that if I continued walking bent over the way I was I would be bowing down to *avodah zarah* (idols), and that that was the reason they had brought me here. I understood that I had about one second to decide what I was going to do.

"I turned around and looked downwards as if I had dropped something on the floor by mistake. Then I searched the floor attempting to find the thing that I thought I had dropped. The whole time that I looked, I backed into the building until the ceiling had straightened out and I was able to stand normally without bowing down. Then and only then did I turn around.

"The two monks were staring at me, and if looks could kill ...." Yacov let the thought hang there for a moment.

"Then I began the investigation.

"About a month later, the letter arrived. It was from the Vatican and it was addressed to the head of the Israeli police force. The letter was not a happy one. It was written in very aggressive form and it claimed that one Israeli police officer, Yacov Pinchasi, had shown brazen disrespect to the Christian religion when he came to the monastery to investigate a break-in that they had experienced. The letter went on to say that the Vatican considered this officer's behavior a disgrace to the entire Israeli police department and that they would consider nothing less then this officer's instant dismissal from the Beit Shemesh force. Otherwise, the letter went on, the Vatican would be extremely displeased, and did the Israeli police department really want to be the cause of a possible breakdown in relations between the two countries? The letter continued on in that way for a while, and the chief of police was understandably shaken up. What was not so understandable was his reaction.

"It seemed that he was going to accede to the Vatican's demands. His orders were passed down from rank to rank until they reached my immediate superior who called me into his office and dressed me down. Then he informed me that even though I had served on the force for twenty years and was a terrific and devoted officer, the force was letting me go without a pension. I was to be put on trial by the in-house police court system and they would make the final decision, but this was pretty much the way that it was going to be. So I was put on trial, judged by my peers and found guilty, and that was the end of everything—twenty years of my life over, just like that. I received 70,000 shekels in compensation and that was the end of my career with the Israeli police force."

We arrive at my house, and Yacov puts the taxi in park. He looks me in the eyes and says: "So now, here I am driving a taxi for a living, while my former partner Amram was able to retire with his pension." Then he continues, wagging his finger at me, "But you should know that if I would be put in the same situation again, knowing that this was going to happen, I would do exactly the same thing all over again!"

We say good-bye and I shake his hand and wish him the best of luck, and as he drives away, I think to myself that there are those who acquire their portion in the World to Come in one hour, and that maybe, just maybe, that was Yacov's hour.

WHAT THE
TAXI DRIVER
told us ...

BY SUSAN SCHWARTZ

Not being accustomed to riding in taxis in the United States, I don't really know if the experience of driving with an Israeli taxi driver is so unique, but it certainly seems so to me. When you're in Israel, you become part of the greater community; the concept of "*kol Yisrael areivim zeh lazeh*—all Jews are responsible for one another" finds constant expression. Storekeepers have no compunction about giving you unsolicited advice, and taxi drivers consider it their faithful duty to become involved in your life.

This was not our first trip to Israel, nor was it the first time we went traveled in Israel by cab. Maybe it was just me—that I was more open to seeing beyond the superficial, but somehow I learned a lot from the taxi drivers this time.

With four of us in the cab, my husband would sit up front with the driver. After negotiating our fare and destination, the driver would ask (in Hebrew, of course) where we were from.

"United States ... Chicago. Have you heard of it?"

Most often, New York was the only city they could name, so they would go on to the next question. "Are you Chassidish? Chabad? Tzioni?" My husband's standard answer was, "*Ani Yehudi ragil*—I'm just a regular Jew."

It was when one of our cab drivers, Gabi, turned to my husband and answered with vehemence that I started to pay close attention. "There is no such thing as a regular Jew!" he said. "All Jews are special—we are all the children of Hashem!"

He went on to elaborate about the importance of family (informing us that he is one of nine and has four children himself, and then asking how many we have), the beauty of children around the Shabbat table, and the legacy we Jews leave to our children through our rituals and observances. He admonished us for not appreciating the seriousness of our tasks as parents and the important role we play in the future of the Jewish people.

My husband and I chuckled afterwards about the friendliness of the driver (in fact, we hired him subsequently for a longer trip and spent a great deal of time discussing the holiness of Eretz Yisrael with him), but we were quickly absorbed in our Yerushalayim experience and didn't give it much further thought.

While we were sitting with our children in a Yerushalayim restaurant, I asked my husband where he wanted to be buried when the time came—Israel or America. After almost choking on his food (my children found the whole conversation hysterical and were busy trying to figure out what "*yerushah*" we would leave them), he said he really couldn't decide. Wouldn't it depend on where the children lived? I told him I thought that if we couldn't get to Israel while we were still alive and able to enjoy it, shouldn't we at the very least be buried there? This prompted a long discussion that ended with no real resolution, since thinking in the abstract is so difficult, and neither of us was ready to buy cemetery plots on that trip. (Although I would guess it has to be a whole lot cheaper than putting a deposit down on an apartment there!)

Then along came the next loquacious cab driver. This time, after asking where we were from and sharing his personal history (he came from Iran), he turned to my husband and said, "Why are you not living here in Israel?"

We gave the usual answer—we would love to, of course, but practically speaking there are so many factors in the equation. He would not give up. "Don't you know that your *parnassah* is from Hashem? Whatever you will have is decided on Rosh Hashanah. Your job is to come here, and Hashem will provide." I was somewhat taken aback. The driver had no *kippah* on his head, and yet he spoke with such authority and intensity about Hashem's role in our lives.

When we got out of the cab, I turned to my husband and said, "Maybe we've been missing the point. Hashem sends messengers to us in all kinds of ways .... Perhaps all these cab drivers have been sent to tell us something. Maybe we need to really hear what they are saying—not just chuckle at the experience." Gabi was right. There is no such thing as a "regular" Jew. We are each unique and have been put here to complete a specific task. We don't always know what our task is, but it is our responsibility to not give up the quest, no matter how bumpy the ride may be along the way.

It is almost a year since that trip. We have not yet bought cemetery plots (although I did enter a raffle for two plots in Israel, figuring it was not the kind of prize too many people would jump for), but I still hope that we will make it to Israel standing upright, ready to tell the next cab driver that we have come home.

FOR THIS CHILD
I PRAYED

TRIUMPH

BY RACHEL LEVINE

*T*he Talmud speaks of a rabbi, Rav Pereida, who had to teach his pupil everything over and over again, four hundred times, until he finally understood it. As a child, I was unfamiliar with this Talmudic vignette. Instead, I was taught the English version: If at first you don't succeed, try, try again. In other words—don't give up hope; it's so easy to sink into despair after repeated failures.

I've wondered about the qualities that propel Down Syndrome children. They have a driving force that is not to be taken for granted. I, for one, am always in awe of my daughter, Tamar's, perseverance.

Eleven-year-old Tamar is overweight, hypotonic and sluggish. Her physical therapist said that exercise was imperative. I wanted to find her a source of exercise that would be stimulating, and one that she could do independently. I thought that jumping rope would be ideal. But, as we say in Yiddish, "*Vi azoi kumpt di katz iber di vasser?* (How does the cat go over the water?)"

One afternoon, Tamar called out, "Ima, come here!" I saw her looking out the window. She pointed at some girls playing jump rope in the parking lot. "I want to play with the girls."

I didn't know what to answer. On the one hand, I was delighted that she took the initiative to play with non-challenged children. But I was afraid that the girls would reject Tamar and thereby hurt her feelings. Nevertheless, my sixth sense urged me to let her go.

Downstairs, I told the girls that Tamar wanted to join them, and that she knew how to turn the rope. Children usually hate turning the rope, so they were delighted at my offer. I decided against asking them to allow Tamar to jump so as not to put them in an awkward position.

Tamar came home, beaming. I held my breath, eager to hear her story. "Ima, I want to play with the girls everyday." I slowly exhaled, relieved and happy that she'd had a good time.

One day, my grandchildren came to visit. Now, *they* were really pros at jumping rope. Tamar pleaded, "I also want to jump."

After Tamar had several failed attempts, the kids gave up. "It doesn't matter, Tamar," they said. "You can try again another time. Now, turn the rope."

Tamar's shoulders slumped, eyes downcast. She began sucking her thumb as she sometimes does when upset or bored. But not for long. Tamar perked up and followed the children outside.

The girls in the parking lot eventually let Tamar jump, but to no avail. I felt terrible when she'd call me, "Ima, see, I can jump," and then not succeed. "*Ooof,* I can't. Look again. *Ooof,* it doesn't work."

"Tamar, you have to see when the rope reaches your feet and then jump." She tried so hard, but succeeded with only one or two jumps. With thumb in mouth, she walked away and occupied herself with something else.

Two months later, we visited one of my married children. My grandchildren took a jump rope and ran off to the patio. Soon after, Tamar ran over, lay her head on my shoulder and burst into tears.

"Tamar, what happened?" I asked. "Did someone hit you? Did you fall?"

Through her sobs, I could barely make out what had happened. She choked on her words, "They … won't … let me jump. They … say … I don't know how to jump."

What I was afraid of finally happened. I was upset and angry. Tamar has a heart just like everyone else, if not more sensitive. It took a lot of willpower not to scold my grandchildren; I didn't want to make a scene in front of them. The parents blushed and squirmed uneasily in their chairs. *Let their parents take care of them,* I thought. It was challenging enough to discipline my own children—I didn't have to discipline my grandchildren, too. I stroked Tamar's head. "Don't worry. *B'ezras Hashem,* you'll learn how to jump rope."

My mother, who had come along with us, looked at me with pained eyes. "Rachel, I'm going to buy Tamar a jump rope. Tatti and I will come over and teach her how to jump." She pressed her lips together in determination.

The following day my parents arrived with a green jump rope. I'll never forget the sight of my old, aged parents teaching a young retarded child to jump rope.

"Tamar, good. You can do it. Wonderful. Again," my father cheered.

"Ima," Tamar said, "I jumped seven times."

"I'm so proud of you. You see, I said you'll learn to jump."

"Ima, Tatti," I said to my parents, "you're something. I can't get over what you've done. Such patience … thank you so much."

On the following Shabbos, I had a bunch of grandchildren on the porch.

"How about jumping rope with Tamar?" I asked. They agreed. A few minutes later, a red-cheeked Tamar rushed into the room with eight smiling children in tow. "Savta, Tamar jumped sixteen times!"

I hugged Tamar. "Wow, that's great."

I said to the children, "Thanks, you're terrific. You have no idea how important this is for Tamar." And quietly to myself: *Thank You, Hashem, for giving me such wonderful parents.*

I wrote a note to Tamar's teacher mentioning her success. I suggested that the school buy a rope for the children to use during recess. That way everyone could benefit. I hadn't received any response, so I dropped the matter.

At the P.T.A. meeting we had three weeks later, the movement therapist looked at me intently and said, "You can't imagine how much good came through your idea. Until now, the staff didn't know that Tamar could jump rope. I wanted to tell you personally what a difference it has made to her self-esteem. She walks with her head high and mopes less. Keep up the good work."

I felt like Rav Pereida in the Talmud, and I understood now. Never give up.

Fostering
LOVE

BY MIKIMI STEINBERG

*T*here are people who are fortunate to grow up in loving and nurturing families, and as such, they know how to bestow this love onto others. They have learned first-hand what *chessed* (kindness) is all about and have cultivated this *middah* (trait) in everything they do, even going out of their way to do more than most people would ever dream of.

This is the story of one such family that I met recently.

The Cohen family (not their real name) live in Eretz Yisrael and have several children, ranging in age from five to fourteen, all, *baruch Hashem,* healthy and happy with their lot in life. And yet, after reading in several magazine articles about the Ben-Baruchs of Tzfat and their remarkable lives raising foster children with Down Syndrome, they, too, felt that taking in such a child, a Down Syndrome baby, was something they could do. It was an idea that would forever change their lives.

The Cohens discussed the idea with their children. The children were intrigued and excited at the prospect of a new baby in the home. They also contacted the Ben-Baruchs of Tzfat to learn from them and were directed on how to proceed on their journey to becoming a foster family. Initially, their *rav* advised them to hold off on their dream for a few years, but finally he gave his approval and blessings.

Calls were made to the social services in their city. Subsequent interviews with each member of the family were completed, as well as several course meetings for the parents, and plenty of forms were filled out. Then the Cohens were added to the list of prospective parents. They waited, and waited.

The Cohens waited an entire year. They dreamed of having the privilege to raise a Down Syndrome child, who, despite the negative label, is usually, by nature, happy-go-lucky and always smiling. Mrs. Cohen even had a dream after davening at a *kever* for just such a child. She dreamt she was on a boat with another, younger woman, and of a big fish. In Yiddishkeit, fish are a sign of fertility. This was a sign to her that soon they would be privileged to have another child join their family.

Finally, the phone call from social services came informing them that there was a baby in a hospital out of town. He was born premature, at just twenty-five weeks. His birth mother did not feel capable of raising a child "born too soon." She had named him "Shai" (gift) and left the hospital. He also had many problems that had not been attended to properly, including hydrocephalus (water on the brain). And he was considered "special needs."

The Cohens immediately went to "retrieve" their son, now three months old. Theirs was a complete and utter love at first sight for this baby who had been abandoned but was now theirs to claim as their own.

The Cohens wrapped up their precious little gift and took him home to meet the rest of the family. The children all clamored and fought for a chance to hug him, hold him and love him.

Their journey as foster parents and a foster family has only just begun. There were several medical obstacles to overcome, but none of the challenges have deterred the Cohens. They are in it for the long haul, whatever that entails.

The *chessed* they are doing is on a daily, hour-by-hour, minute-by-minute basis. When it's our own child, we don't think twice about the bother involved. But when it's another person's baby, there is room for questions, for doubts. Not so with the Cohens. Shai is theirs, their gift, forever.

SWEET
NACHAS

BY DEVORAH LIFSHUTZ

O n the first day of Chanukah this year, my children surprised me by becoming the people I hoped they would be. It happened quite unexpectedly amid circumstances that I would not have seen as conducive to the achievement of great spiritual heights.

The story began when a relative came for dinner on the first night of the holiday. Wishing to please our children and to be a good guest, he brought along gifts—large cellophane bags stuffed with candies of every imaginable color, shape and flavor. We sat down to eat and our guest noticed that meat was on the menu.

"The candies are dairy. Better put them away and save them," Uncle Bill said to me. "Give them out tomorrow and tell them I brought them."

The following afternoon, I suddenly remembered Uncle Bill and the candy.

"Kids," I called, "we've got a special Chanukah present from our guest last night. I want to give it to you now."

All the children from the oldest, aged eleven, to the youngest, aged three, gathered round the dining room table in eager antici-pation as I distributed the bags.

One of the children poured his out onto the dining room table. There were tiny chocolate bars, small caramel squares, lico-rice sticks with pink and white filling, and even a jelly candy made to look like a pair of dentures.

The kids were floating to paradise, but before anyone could

pop anything in their mouth, eleven-year-old Yossi brought us back down to earth.

"Ima, are you sure those candies are kosher?"

"Oh, my gosh!" He was right.

When Uncle Bill presented me with the treats, I was too busy frying latkes in the kitchen to check where they had come from. Fortunately, there was a phone number printed below the name of the store. I dialed and made the necessary inquiries. Sadly, the answers were not to my liking.

Much to my amazement, most of the children simply gave me back the bags.

That just made my day. All the tantrums, all the scolding, all the breaking up of fights, all the sleepless nights and prayers and labor pains, all the sweat, tears and toil that I had poured into these children were not in vain. They were growing up to be people I could be proud of and people who would bring *nachas* to their Creator.

Now that was quite enough to put me on cloud nine, but then Yossi said something that I think hit the spiritual jackpot.

"Everybody," he said with the utmost urgency in his young voice, "please don't say a word to Uncle Bill. This will hurt his feelings. This is all a secret."

I had just learned of the extreme care our rabbis had taken to avoid inflicting any kind of emotional distress, and here was my own son showing this kind of sensitivity. My other children immediately agreed to the pact of silence.

Now I was faced with the problem of what to do with the candy. I assumed that I'd just dump it in the trash.

"Take them back to the store, Ima, and exchange them," said seven-year-old Shiah.

"But they aren't wrapped. I don't think the store will want them," I explained.

"Try," he insisted.

The following day, I happened to be near the candy store. Much to my amazement, the clerk took the sweets, weighed them and told me their cash worth. I was then free to exchange them for anything in the store that caught my fancy.

To me, this, too, was a miracle.

After considerable deliberation and quite a bit of squinting over microscopic kosher signs, I came up with the consolation prize: a super-sized "Glatt" kosher atomizer that shpritzed sweet liquid directly onto the tongue and something non-caloric, a space-aged looking spinning top that lit up as it spun and played "*sevivon sov, sov, sov.*" I bought one of each for each child. *Identical gifts to avoid jealousy*, I thought.

That night after candle-lighting, I distributed the substitute prizes.

The reviews were mixed. The younger children liked the atomizers. The older ones found them revolting. Some of the tops were sturdy; others broke on the second or third spin. The cries, shrieks and complaints made everything feel back to normal.

But then again, isn't that life? One step forward and two steps back. Even amid the screams and cries and shrieks, I shall try to hold that precious moment in my mind when my young children proved that doing Hashem's will was far more valuable to them than even a bag full of candy.

Best
FRIENDS

BY JUDY GRUENFELD

When we are born, no one knows which road lies before us. We could be inundated with material goods or barely eke out a living. We could be what society deems good-looking, or we could have a face "only a mother could love." We could be blessed with good health or be stricken with a dreadful disease. We could also have many healthy, happy, normal children (*kayn ayin hara*), or we could be blessed by one who is not as "perfect" as his contemporaries.

The gift of a disabled child comes in various wrappings, unraveling all our hopes and dreams as the paper is torn away. Suddenly, the future is not so clear. What will happen to this child? How will the world treat him? What will happen when I am no longer here? He has siblings who love him, but they must lead their own lives.

But if we take advantage of the many resources around us, life will be much more fulfilling for all those involved in our special child's life. For me, until recently, that resource was my parents. My father is the best father a girl could have and the best grandfather my son could have.

From day one, Grandpa and Ronnie were inseparable. They are best friends of the highest order. As Ronnie once put it, "Grandpa loves me best."

Ronnie always liked lights. That is why Grandpa held him up to the light switches when he was a baby and Ronnie turned the lights on and off as he giggled with delight. They went for walks, they played ball; Grandpa read to Ronnie until Ronnie could read, and then they took turns reading to each other. When my parents stayed over, Ronnie snuggled in bed with them, drowning in their kisses.

So last spring, when my father was told he needed open-heart surgery for a clogged coronary artery and a calcified heart valve, Ronnie was devastated. Ronnie can certainly relate to hearts. He's got one of the best ones I've encountered.

I'll never forget one particular Friday afternoon, when he was five years old. Ronnie and I were walking down Clifton Avenue when an elderly lady in front of us tripped and fell to the ground. My little *tzaddik* tried to pick her up while asking, "Are you all right?"

The lady told me she had never seen such a small child show such compassion for another person. Ronnie is considered perceptually impaired, often a given with many developmental disabilities, but I often wonder just whose perception it is that is impaired. I believe that he often sees things more clearly than the rest of us.

Baruch Hashem, my father is doing fine. Ronnie has, of course, been to visit him often, and I believe these visits have been an integral part of my father's successful recovery.

Ronnie and my father were, are and always will be best friends.

SUCCESS
 *Story*

BY SHIFRA COHEN

"**K**ids at risk" has become a huge concern for all parents and is a major issue today. I would like to share with you the saga saga of my son Yossi, if you'll step back with me in time some twenty-five years or so. Perhaps hearing of my experience will be helpful and encouraging to other parents who may find themselves in a similar situation.

Yossi was not doing well in school. He was tutored all along and still had a hard time keeping up with his schoolwork. I was constantly being called in by the principal. It was not a happy situation.

Today, with many thanks to Hashem, Yossi is married to his *ezer k'negdo* with, *ka"h*, several children. He is an exemplary husband and father, responsible and caring. He's running a successful business and, *baruch Hashem*, is doing beautifully. He learns three hours daily, morning and evening. He even learns with a prominent *rav* in his community!

We were his advocates from day one. He knew from the very start how much we cared for him. And even in the most difficult of times, we were his primary advocates. *Baruch Hashem*, we focused on all his wonderful positive traits, and with Hashem's help, he came through with flying colors.

I made a point of getting to know the teachers before problems arose. Having a friendly working relationship with the teachers made it somewhat easier to deal with the challenges that arose.

I was called in to meet the principal fairly regularly those days. Eventually, I learned to come prepared for the meeting. I was doing my own research on child psychology. I would talk to expert teachers. This way, I was not on the defensive when we met. I was an equal partner in the discussion. I refused to be intimidated. I would read up and write notes on points that I wanted to make. I would refer to my papers throughout the meeting. I really had to psych myself up before each meeting. If not for this prep, I would have just dissolved into a bundle of tears as the principal began his tirade. Then and now, I do not think the principal handled him properly at all. He was totally at a loss with this young man, who truly possessed so many wonderful traits. By preparing myself, by being proactive, I was emotionally in a much better state, better able to deal with the principal, as well as deal with my son.

Yossi was a real "people person," and we worked hard to cultivate all his natural talents. Although scholastically challenged at the time, nevertheless, he always had a sunny, winning personality. He was the one who befriended the older men in *shul*, and they in turn adored him. He was the one who taught the little boys how to ride a two-wheeler. When he began to drive, he became the family chauffeur. He was a real entrepreneur and began making money at a very young age. He was a natural and a bright boy. He knew the make and specifics of every car that had been manufactured over the previous twenty years. Within our large circle of family and friends, he knew exactly who was driving which car and for how long. He knew the names of all the baseball players and their statistics.

For some reason though, when it came to formal schoolwork, his head was elsewhere. He was also terrific with his hands and was our family handyman. We certainly used his innate talents! He had a beautiful singing voice and was comfortable singing in public. Throughout, we emphasized his enormous gifts and downplayed the rest. Despite his obvious problems within the school setting, he always felt good about himself.

The guidance counselor shared with me one point in particular that gave me tremendous fortitude. "Within the total picture, school is truly a very small part of one's life. In several years, he'll be out of school and will be able to put all this behind him. Being a real 'people person,' he has the skills to make it in the real world, even though these years are so tough for him. Just hold out."

The high school years began, and again we were challenged. The first high school was too much for him; the hours were too long, so we switched him to another *yeshiva*. Both of these *yeshivos* were very small schools, and my husband and I were in constant contact with the *rebbeim* and principals.

Hashem was good to us, and our son developed a beautiful relationship with several of his *rebbeim*, to whom I will always feel a huge debt of gratitude. Even this situation was not ideal; we felt that he wasn't using his time wisely and was not accomplishing enough, and so, with our permission and blessing, he left high school early. My husband went with him to Israel, and together they explored the options available, visiting various *yeshivos* and meeting with the *roshei yeshiva*. Together, they decided upon a small yeshiva, run by a charismatic *rav*. He spent three to four years in that yeshiva and, *baruch Hashem,* did beautifully. He is still very close to his Rosh Yeshiva from Israel and maintains contact with him.

All in all, he is an incredible success story.

I've shared this saga with several young parents who are struggling with their young children today, and I encourage them not to despair. I say, "Advocate for them. Make sure they know that you are with them one-hundred percent. Assure them of your love. Remember that academic excellence is only one part of the picture. Look at your child as a whole, not as a fragmented being. Work on developing his self-esteem. Seek out his innate talents and help him develop in those areas. Do whatever it takes to help him feel good about himself. Encourage friendships with peers. Encourage him to bring home friends; make sure your home is kid-friendly and inviting, warm and fun for him and his friends. And remember always, Hashem is an active partner in raising this child. Include Him in the process. Daven and ask for guidance. Ask for patience, stamina and fortitude."

May Hashem bless us all with joy and *Yiddishe nachas*.

The names in this story have been changed.

DIVINE ORCHESTRATION

THE RAREST of GIFTS

BY SARA DEBBIE GUTFREUND

She grasps the side of the rough, gray rock that juts out of the cliff towering above her. Glancing back at her hiking partner, she can see that her friend regrets following her down this trail, but they are almost at the top now.

When they scramble over the last steep patch of rocks, they see that the top of the mountain is deserted. Hills, the color of deep azure, stretch into a sea of greenery all around them. She is intoxicated with the accomplishment of having climbed so high. Her friend is not as enthralled. She shifts nervously on her feet, anxious about climbing down.

Suddenly, they hear a soft groan, and she spots a person lying about fifteen feet away from them. As they come closer, they see that an elderly man is bleeding profusely from his forehead. His white beard is streaked with blood.

"I fell and hit my head on a rock," he mumbles in a weak voice. For a moment, they stand beside him, paralyzed with the panic of helplessness. Then she remembers the cell phone in her knapsack.

"You think it will work all the way up here?" she asks her friend.

"It's worth a try," she answers as she looks up the emergency number on the hiking map pamphlet. Thousands of feet in the air, the cell phone works. The dispatcher tells them that he's sending a helicopter and that they should try to control the bleeding.

She finds an extra shirt in her knapsack, and her friend begins ripping it into makeshift bandages. They work together with trembling hands, wondering how this flimsy shirt is going to stop the stream of blood flowing from the man's head.

Just then a heavyset woman lumbers up the side of the mountain and, shading her eyes from the afternoon sun, she shouts above the wind.

"You guys okay over there?"

"This man is badly hurt," her friend cries back. The woman rushes over and grabs the shirt. She begins expertly tearing bandages and pressing them onto the man's head.

"I'm an emergency nurse," she explains as she checks his vital signs. Then they hear another voice behind them, deep and concerned.

"What happened?" A tall man in hiking gear is making his way toward them. After examining the injured man's head, he explains that he is a neurosurgeon. He helps the nurse stabilize the bleeding.

Soon the helicopter roars above them, and they crouch next to the rocks as it lands. As the emergency workers bring the injured man into the helicopter, the sun begins to set. All around them the hills are aflame with the majesty of Hashem. And she begins to count the ways that Hashem took care of that injured hiker: the cell phone, the extra shirt in her knapsack, the emergency nurse, the neurosurgeon and the rescue helicopter. All on a deserted mountaintop. And then she begins to count the ways that Hashem takes care of her. And she finds that there are so many ways, day after day, that she can't begin to count them.

As she watches the helicopter disappear into the darkening sky, she bows her head in awe. Look how Hashem orchestrates our lives. How He sends messengers to heal our wounds. How He guides us up mountains and carries us down.

There, on that empty mountaintop with her head cradled in her arms, she receives the rarest of gifts. Hashem makes her aware that He takes care of her. And since that day, there is a person hidden inside of her who is still kneeling on the rocks with her head in her arms, thanking Hashem for every minute of her day.

DIVINE
WAKE-UP *Call*

BY MARY KROPMAN

*I*t had been a busy day in the trading store serving the black customers small amounts of tea, sugar, flour and other household necessities. The next day was New Year's, 1953, and the customers knew that the doors would be closed. They came from near and far to make their small purchases. The children would put out their tiny black hands and beg for a *basella*. They would clap with joy for the few sticky sweets they received. The shop would be filled with their chatter and constant clicks of the Xhosa language.

Auntie Esther and I were in charge while my parents took a cruise on a Union Castle Line ship. I was pleased that I could assist in the shop while they had a holiday; they worked so hard throughout the year and seldom took holidays. However, how I wished I could be smelling the salty sea breeze instead of being stuck in the hamlet of Debe Nek. Everyone else was going to the party at the hotel down the road. We never went to the parties given by the non-Jews. It would be a mixed crowd of traders, farmers and railway and road workers. They were a rowdy lot for whom fun was drinking and brawling.

"I am so tired," I told my aunt. "I want to soak my tired sore feet in some hot water and go to bed." It was easier to take hot water from the stove than heat up the old copper geyser in the bathroom.

Auntie Esther and I shared a room adjoining the shop. The fragrance of the peach blossoms wafted into the room through the open window. The only light was from the candle on the oak table. We both soon fell asleep. I awoke with a start; the room except for a small ray of moonlight was as black as our coal stove. What had awakened me? I then heard sounds coming from the shop, boxes and tins falling. I was shivering, and at the same time perspiration was forming on my brow. I could hear my heart THUMPING against my chest. "Maybe it's only a cat," I thought to myself. However, the sounds of falling articles continued. It grew quiet until I heard the chaffing of the sash window in the room opposite the bedroom. This was no cat but a burglar who was soon busy eating and drinking in the kitchen.

Next he went into my parents' bedroom. We could hear him tampering with the huge heavy iron safe. The footsteps were coming toward our room, and my heart felt as though it was in my throat. We were terrified; neither of us had uttered a word since the onset of this drama. We had nothing with which we could protect ourselves — my father's gun was locked in the safe. The only help would be a miracle performed by the Almighty. I said to myself, "Please, Hashem, don't let us come to any harm." The footsteps were almost at our door when a sudden shrill sound pierced the air. Where did the loud incessant sound come from? A loud crash sounded as the burglar knocked over a chair as he hurriedly retraced his steps and climbed through the open window.

We waited a few minutes and then dashed to the telephone in the adjoining room where the alarm clock on the mantelpiece was ringing. We turned the handle of the telephone repeatedly — no reply. On the floor was a huge butcher's knife, which the burglar must have dropped in his fright. The ringing of the old clock on the mantelpiece had saved us. It could only be *Yad Hashem*.

When day broke, we walked to the hotel down the dusty path strewn with all kinds of clothing and groceries from the shop. The bleary-eyed hotel manager answered our persistent ringing on the front door. We related the story and told him that we could not be connected to the police station, as our telephone was out of order. He took us to the switchboard next to the pub. He apologized profusely, "The party got out of hand and some of the young guys fooling around made random phone calls, awakening the neighbors, and that is when the partygoers must have ripped out all the lines." He connected the lines, and we telephoned the nearest police station in the next village.

The police and their snuffer dogs soon arrived. A young prisoner awaiting trial had recently escaped, and they suspected him. They were able to trace him to a nearby farm where he was hiding. Auntie Esther received a summons to appear in court. The magistrate asked whether she recognized the man in the dock. She replied, "Mr. Magistrate, him I don't know, but his trousers I do know. The trousers belong to my son. You can see for yourself a patch on the knees. If you look at the lining of the pockets you will see that they are as green as grass." The prisoner was made to show the inside of his pockets, and they were bright green! Auntie Esther had not only patched the trousers but she had made them! She continued to relate the story of the burglary, and when the burglar heard about the ringing of the clock, he was furious. Auntie Esther said that he looked as if he could have killed her, then and there. Nobody could believe how the clock had saved us. I knew that it was Divine Providence.

This clock was a small white Westclock, which we took into the shop in the day and brought into the house at closing time. That day I had played with the alarm. I realized that the fact that I had played with the clock, and in doing so had set the alarm, was a miracle. It was Hashem who guided me to play with the clock and made it ring at midnight, at the exact moment that we needed the burglar to be frightened away. *Hodu laHashem ki tov, ki l'olam chasdo* (Give thanks to Hashem for He is good; His kindness endures forever).

ROLLER *coaster*

BY SHEINDEL DEVORAH BAS MIRIAM

"It's like being on a roller coaster," I sighed, as I explained to a friend how being diagnosed with cancer was affecting me. The days were rushing by in a blur as I went through test after test, days of waiting and praying for good results. Days of exhilaration from good news, followed by dismay from bad news, then good news again, then bad, doctors who said it's not that bad, doctors who said it was worse than the previous doctor implied—first opinions, second opinions, third opinions, on and on, up and down, back and forth, upside down. It's a roller coaster ... and I am the type who sticks to the merry-go-round at the amusement park!

"Close your eyes!" rabbis, friends, family told me. Finally, I did it; I stopped looking up for a cure, down for a prognosis. I stopped trying to figure out how I would get myself out of this mess because I wasn't going to. Hashem was.

I closed my eyes in deep prayer and trusted Hashem to take care of me and give me the strength to live out my life according to His plan. Once I did that, I wasn't dizzy anymore, and the world stopped whizzing by in a blur.

There are still ups and downs, but it's more like a safe and calming merry-go-round ride, with pretty music playing if I take time to listen.

Helpless...
and *Loving It*

BY SUSAN SCHWARTZ

"Everyone is staring at me," my daughter wailed.

It's hard to give comfort over the phone when you're 5,000 miles away, but I did my best to sound wise and caring. On her own for the first time, our daughter seemed to be adapting well to the Israel seminary experience. She had made friends with her roommates, was experiencing the thrills of walking in Yerushalayim each day and even found some of her classes to be mildly interesting (a great comfort to her parents, who were spending so much money for the experience).

One week into this idyllic life (what can be bad when your parents are sending you money?), the school took their first trip. A laughing Huvi called to tell me she had fallen down a rocky hillside while climbing, and—klutzily—probably sprained her ankle. Joining in her laughter (after all, she inherited the "klutz gene" from me), I told her to ice her ankle and take a painkiller when she returned to her dorm.

But the laughter turned to tears when she called a few hours later from the emergency room to tell me the ankle was actually broken, that she was in a cast up to her knee, and that she couldn't put any weight on her ankle for six weeks.

Surprised at the severity of the injury, I tried to calm her worries, and called friends and family in Israel to ask that they try to comfort her and help her out. Her roommates helped with her laundry, and carrying her books to class. Friends invited her for *yamim tovim* and helped her to get a wheelchair, and now, in the middle of Sukkos, she was calling me to cry about how much she hated being a public spectacle.

I certainly didn't want to belittle the physical discomfort she was going through, nor did a pat answer like, "Don't worry, it's just a few more weeks," seem like the right thing to say under the circumstances. But suddenly I was inspired with something to say.

"Huvi," I said, "just look at what Hashem has done for you! You've always wanted to work with handicapped and sick children, and now you've been given an opportunity to really feel what they go through. You feel like everyone stares at you in your wheelchair; you hate having to impose on your friends to help you get up and down the stairs and accomplish the everyday tasks you took for granted. You have pain in your arms and hands from supporting yourself on crutches. But all that will go away. Your experiences, though—your memories of these feelings—will never go away, and they'll be there for you to call on when you work with these kids. Now you have a taste of the *nisyonos* (trials) that they have to go through each day. Your *nisayon* is temporary, *baruch Hashem*. But this experience will be with you forever."

If this were an episode of "Father Knows Best," that would have been the end of it. A tearful "Kitten" would smile at her father, recognizing these great words of wisdom. Real life doesn't always work that way, though. Huvi did not seem all that consoled by my words. So I tried again, this time using humor. "Okay, then, put a cup on your lap and call out '*tzedakah*'—if everyone's really staring at you like you think, I bet you'll actually collect some money for charity."

That at least elicited some laughter.

For the next few weeks, our phone bills mounted as Huvi called to cry and sometimes laugh at her various experiences as a temporarily handicapped person. Finally the day arrived—the x-rays were examined and the cast came off. Returning to walk did not come easily, though, and for a while she still needed crutches and physical therapy to regain her mobility.

Some day, *im yirtzeh Hashem*, Huvi will work with handicapped children. In spite of what she may think now, I know she will look back at this experience as one that helped to increase her natural empathy, and she'll realize that she passed her test with flying colors.

HASHEM'S MESSENGERS

A WILDFLOWER GARDEN *for the* Neighborhood

BY PAULA R. STEEN

"*H*ey!" A man yelled at me out of his car window one morning last summer. "Great garden!" I was standing on the sidewalk in front of my house picking dead heads off the bachelor buttons growing between the sidewalk and curb. I turned around, but he just drove on.

A week later, a woman carrying a violin case walked by with her young daughter. "So pretty flowers," she said in accented English. "We are from Ukraine. They grow there. It reminds me."

"They grow wild in the field there," her daughter added in pure "Americanese."

By then the bachelor buttons were four feet tall, the yarrow had reached its brightest white and my California and corn poppies were straggling over the curb. Even the zinnias were beginning to have blossoms. In fact, the woman next door came out, snapped pictures of the profusion and gave me copies.

Amazing, I thought, how a wildflower garden in the city surprises people and lures them into moments of companionship. For five years we had lived in our condo in Brookline, just outside of Boston, but knew few people on the street. Our lives revolved around our jobs, our children, and our friends in the *shul* we attended. Although 50 percent of Brookline's residents are Jewish, with a large Orthodox population, we seldom saw religious garb on our street. People here were polite, but distant. The wildflowers changed that.

At first I couldn't understand it; there are lots of nice gardens in town. When I walk home from the trolley, I pass townhouse after condo where people have planted, or have hired others to plant, carefully-tended groups of daffodils, and where tulips grow in the spring and impatiens or pansy flowers blossom in the summer.

My garden was an afterthought in comparison. I had just picked up some packages of wildflower seeds in March while I was waiting at the checkout line in the hardware store. All you had to do, the package said, was rake over the ground an inch or so deep, mix the seeds with some soil, scatter the mixture over the planting area, scatter more soil on top, press it in and water it regularly. That seemed easy enough.

So, in April, I followed the instructions. In front of our condo between the sidewalk and the curb, in a space about 2½ feet across and 22 feet long, I planted my wildflower garden. For weeks nothing happened. Then some little green things started poking out of the soil.

"You'd better pick those weeds," my husband said.

"No! What if they're flowers? Don't wildflowers grow like weeds?"

They grew taller and taller and still looked like weeds. I decided to give my garden another week to prove it was a garden and not just a swarm of weeds. Then, about two months after I'd planted the seeds, flat clusters of white flowers appeared on one of the stems above feathery leaves.

Several mornings later, as I stood on the street pulling out grass—the only other thing I could recognize that was definitely not flowers—a woman walked by with her dog.

"Your yarrow is looking good," she said.

Around the yarrow, blue and pink and white flowers soon appeared on grayish-blue stems. As I watered them one evening a bicyclist stopped. "You should pick off the dead heads on those bachelor buttons," he said, "if you want them to keep blooming." He remounted and peddled away. I started pulling off the wilted blossoms.

"That's great cosmos you have there," a runner said a few days later, stopping and taking off his Walkman. He told me about the garden his mother had in the Midwest, where cosmos lined the fence in front of the house. He put his Walkman back on and continued down the street.

As summer drew to a close, the flowers continued to bloom. I found myself stepping out to the curb every morning and evening and sometimes in between, just to enjoy the colors, the bees, the butterflies and my chats with the neighbors. I discovered that our neighbors on the left are Jewish, and two houses down there's an Israeli couple who anxiously wait for weekly reports from their son in the IDF. The Ukrainian woman with the violin case, stopping by now and then, wanted her daughter to have opportunities in America that had been denied people of Jewish descent in her country.

"Are those wildflowers?" a jogger demanded at the end of August. Taking a break and a drink from her water bottle, she gazed at the poppies I had planted among the bachelor buttons. "Where did you get them?"

"I planted them."

"From seed?"

"Yes."

"I don't believe it!"

She seemed sincerely amazed. We talked a few minutes and then, as she continued on her way, she called over her shoulder, "Thank you for making the street more beautiful."

I watched her disappear, and then hurried into the house to get my car keys. I knew I'd need to have lots of mulch on hand when it started getting cold.

It occurred to me that it's so easy for us to withdraw into our homes, our circle of friends, our jobs, and turn our backs on others. But as we tend our gardens, we also tend our community. As our plants grow, we grow, too, learning to care about those who might otherwise have simply passed us by.

In November, I ordered wildflower catalogues. What a selection! I wasn't sure if I should do bachelor buttons again. I wondered what the neighbors would like best. After all, it would be their garden as much as mine.

The Bar
MITZVAH

BY MANUEL SAND

*T*he possibility of conferring *chessed* on a rich person is a rarely realized opportunity for a performer of *chessed*. Often, it is only in retrospect that we discover we have been able to fulfill this mitzvah to the amazement and appreciation of all concerned.

Such an opportunity fell into my lap inadvertently some thirty years ago.

The year 1975 was a regular one in the life insurance business, and I was busy managing the company, which was my occupation for some twenty years.

Among the many activities in which I participated at the time, I was very active in the Insurance Brokers Association, promoting the position of the agent in Israel and working ardently toward increasing the professionalism of the life insurance industry as a whole, and the agent in particular.

The association, at my urging, decided to organize a sales congress to be held in Jerusalem, wherein the agents would participate and learn about sales and other subjects of interest to them. At my suggestion, we invited five of the great life insurance notables of our day, and perhaps of all time.

It was very important for the industry as a whole that we succeed in this endeavor, and among those invited were Ben Feldman, the all-time great super salesman and past president of the M.D.R.T. (million dollar round table), and three other outstanding speakers of worldwide renown. In passing,

I should mention that four of the five were Jewish.

The five accepted the association's invitation, and the sales congress was planned for February. Hotel reservations were made, as were first-class plane reservations. The planning committee took over arranging the program for the congress and sightseeing for the guests and their wives, as well as all the necessary arrangements for holding the congress in Jerusalem. This was no easy task since we were expecting a turnout of over three hundred attendees. Suffice it to say, everything went into high gear to assure the success of the sales congress. The topics and speakers were scheduled and all was prearranged for a successful meeting.

I was asked to serve on the hosting committee for the honored guests. Arrangements were made for welcoming the guests arriving on Friday at the first-class lounge at the airport. The congress was to begin the following Monday.

Just as planned, we greeted the guests with the necessary fanfare and had limousines waiting after their early welcome at Ben Gurion airport. Just before parting for Jerusalem, I announced that my family and I would be staying with them at the Hilton Hotel for Shabbat. I also mentioned that I would be attending Friday evening Shabbat services at The Great Synagogue and that anyone wishing to join me would be able to grab a lift with me at 5:00 p.m. in front of the hotel. We would then walk back after services.

True to my word, I was dutifully parked outside the hotel at the appointed hour and was joined by two of the participants and their wives for our ride to the synagogue.

Our guests were not religious, had never been to Israel and were thrilled to be here for the first time. I might also mention that these were the most successful people in the life insurance industry, all of whom were earning seven-figure incomes.

I parked the car and we entered the synagogue, which

impressed them greatly. They were in awe of the luxurious trappings of the sanctuary. We seated ourselves in the front row, as the women made their way to the upper gallery.

Services began led by the cantor and, sitting between my guests, I found them the page in the *siddur*.

At one point, one of the guests, Ben, bent over and whispered into my ear that he was unable to read Hebrew. I calmed him and said, "That's okay, no problem." The service continued and once again he whispered into my ear that he had never been to *cheder*, was the oldest of six children, had lost his father at a very young age and sold newspapers on the street corner during the Depression to help with the family *parnassah* while his younger brothers and sisters attended Hebrew school. A little further on, he whispered into my ear a third time, "You know, Manny, I didn't even have a bar mitzvah."

Ben, at the time, was over seventy years of age, and I turned to him and said, "Ben, you're in Israel now, and on Monday morning we will be going to the Kotel, the Western Wall, where you will be called up to the Torah."

A tear trickled from his eye as he looked at me and said unbelievingly, "Manny, you mean you will make me a bar mitzvah?"

"Yes," I answered. "We will invite guests, bring cake and liquor, and celebrate your *aliyah* to the Torah as a bar mitzvah this coming Monday morning."

It's hard to put into words the emotions emanating from this man. Suffice it to say, the joy on his face was wonderful to behold!

On our departure from the sanctuary, we met his wife Rosebud descending the stairs, and as they greeted each other he said, "Rosebud, I'm being bar mitzvahed on Monday morning at the Western Wall." They both began to cry tears of joy, and slowly we made our way out of the *shul* toward the street.

We walked to the hotel together, and as we arrived at the Hilton, we were greeted by others on the welcoming committee. Ben dutifully invited all of them to his bar mitzvah.

When he met his colleagues who had arrived with him, one of them approached me with the identical story. I told him that he, too, would also have his bar mitzvah. Soon a third guest came to me with the same story and received from me the same assurance.

From that point onward, the three superstars invited everyone they met to their bar mitzvah, and we were now assured of a respectable crowd for the event.

Needless to say, we had a very nice Shabbat, and on my return to Tel Aviv on Sunday morning, the wheels were put into motion. Esther Ella, my wife, baked some cakes. I put a bridge table, a bottle of scotch and some disposable glasses into the car, and my secretary began searching for bar mitzvah certificates and a calligrapher, all the while informing the media of the forthcoming event.

Monday morning dawned and at 7:30 a.m., we gathered at the Kotel. We davened Shacharit and took out a *sefer Torah*. All the bar mitzvahs were called up to get an *aliyah*, and I must say it was a beautiful and highly emotional event. We had a drink and were all invited to a bar mitzvah reception, which had been arranged at the hotel.

The Israeli breakfast, famous worldwide for its variety of succulent goodies, served as the background for the speeches that followed. Most impressive was the message these giants of industry conveyed to the invited guests:

We had anything money could buy; the only thing we didn't have was a bar mitzvah, and we felt deprived all our lives. Now we have this as well. Thank you for giving us this gift, which we could never have bought for money anywhere.

The sales congress was a huge success, and as a postscript to this story, a few months later I received an invitation to a bar mitzvah celebration in California from Ben and Rosebud, inviting me to their synagogue to celebrate his bar mitzvah among his friends and family.

IT'S
in the BLOOD

AS RELATED TO M. WINNER

Several years ago, I heard about a little boy who was in dire need of blood for the many transfusions he was undergoing for a life-threatening illness, *rachmana litzlan*. Someone from the community was organizing donors to match this boy's blood-recipient identification code to send to donation centers so that they could give blood specifically for him. I told the organizer that I would participate, and I happily went to the local blood bank to take care of it immediately.

Having donated blood numerous times, I was taken aback when before the procedure the nurse asked me if I had by chance been in Europe between the late 1980s and the early 1990s. "I actually lived there during those years," I said surprised, and asked, "Why? I have given blood many times before, and this was never a problem."

She explained that due to outbreaks of mad cow disease in Europe during those years, I was ineligible to give blood not only this time but *forever*—that is, until a cure for mad cow was found. I was devastated! Not only did I want to give blood for this little boy, but I also wanted to continue donating blood for other people since it was a mitzvah I had fortunately always been able to do with ease.

As I prepared to leave, I decided I'd better call the coordinator to tell him what had happened. Dismayed, I entered the waiting area and searched my bag for my cell phone. A young man in a *yarmulke* and *tzitzis* was standing there speaking with the receptionist. "But I have the name, I just don't have the code," he was explaining in vain.

"Sir, as I already made clear, you cannot donate blood for a specific recipient without the code," the receptionist said, about to lose her patience.

"Please, ma'am, I have the name," he tried again. Overhearing this exchange, I approached the young man. "Excuse me," I said. "I just came to donate for a specific kid, too. Perhaps you are here for the same person and I could give you the code?" The names didn't match.

I thought for a moment. "Well, I have the number of a donations coordinator. Perhaps I could call him and see if he has this child's code," I suggested.

Pulling out my cell phone, I called the coordinator. He did not have that code, but he thought he knew someone who did. He said he would call me back in five minutes. As I waited for the phone to ring, I contemplated the idea that perhaps the whole purpose in my being there was to make this very call at this very moment. The ringing phone confirmed it. The coordinator had gotten the code. Even though I hadn't been able to give blood, I was supposed to be there anyway to enable someone else to do so.

Uplifted by this unexpected *hashgachah*, I prepared to hang up. "You should know," the coordinator comforted me, "that the *refuah* is not about the actual blood donation or other similar acts. The *refuah* comes through loving-kindness and *chessed*, like what you just did."

A VISIT *from* ELIYAHU

BY ROSALLY SALTSMAN

Pesach 1950. Seder night in Jaffa.

Avraham and Chaya Coopershlack, religious new immigrants who had barely survived the Holocaust, arrived on Israel's shores in 1948 from Poland after passing through Russia, Germany and the most horrific of the extermination camps. They lived in a small apartment with Chaya's sister and niece and were sharing the Seder night with her brother. Avraham Coopershlack was a shoemaker who had come from generations of shoemakers, but as war refugees, he and his wife had no *parnassah*. Just each other.

Seder night. The small group read from the Hagaddah. They came to the part of *Sh'foch Chamas'cha* and opened the door to receive Eliyahu Hanavi. As they were reciting the passage, there was a knock on the open door. An old woman was standing there with a basket in her hand. She told them that she had nowhere to sleep and asked for a place to rest. In the small apartment, there was no empty bed to give her, but they graciously laid out a blanket for her to sleep on the floor.

Not everyone felt comfortable giving this woman a place to sleep, but who could refuse her request? After the Seder, they all went to bed.

Chaya Coopershlack woke up suddenly just before dawn and tentatively went to check on her guest. The old woman wasn't there. But in her place, she had left the basket she had been carrying. Chaya woke her husband, who ran outside with the basket trying to find the old woman who had left so suddenly and mysteriously. The whole episode seemed very strange to them.

After Pesach, Chaya went out with the empty basket, and as she went about her errands from place to place, she announced that her husband, a shoemaker, was looking for work fixing shoes. Everywhere she went, they gave her shoes to fix. She went out in the morning with an empty basket and returned home with a basket full of shoes that needed mending. And from that day on, *baruch Hashem*, they had *parnassah*.

After a few months, the basket was lost. But the *parnassah* kept coming in and Avraham eventually opened a store. He understood that this old woman had to have been a good messenger, perhaps Eliyahu Hanavi in disguise, and that now the basket had gone to someone else in need of a miracle.

PARTNERS
- In Torah, in Chessed, in Life

BY SHEINDEL WEINBACH

"We're going to drop everything, take out a loan and order tickets to Eretz Yisrael," declared Dina's husband, her Partner in Life. He had never been there in his forty-two years; she had spent a summer there as a teenager. Dropping everything meant respective jobs and figuring out what to do with six school-age kids, and right after Purim, which meant right before Pesach.

"Now? The worst time of the year?" said their rabbi to Dina, his partner in running the *shul* in everything but religious matters. But it was fine with him. After all, he was the one who was urging them to go. "*Chavrusos* go to the weddings of *chavrusos*, no?"

It had all begun three years earlier, when Dina's father passed away, and she finally decided it was time to make the commitment long in the planning: to take on a Partner in Torah. The world-famous Partners in Torah organization paired her off with Sharon on the other side of the U.S., and they began a talking and learning relationship on the phone around March. By Elul, Sharon was ready for a bona fide Rosh Hashanah, and agreed to be hosted by Dina. As a result of that visit, their friendship, which had grown over the months, became firmly cemented, and Sharon, divorced when her only son was a year old, was eager to take on Torah and *mitzvos*. Her son Jim had gone along with this and attended a seminar and subsequent classes. Being a bright, sociable kid with leadership qualities, his mentors suggested that he could best maximize his capabilities in Eretz Yisrael.

Not long after he was settled in yeshiva, Sharon called up Dina breathless with excitement. "Jim has met this girl and says he is getting engaged. Tomorrow!"

Well, that called for action. Dina's husband called up Israel to check up on the match, which sounded great — a London girl from a traditional home studying in a seminary in Israel, with blessings from his and her mentors. And the wedding was planned for a month's time. In Israel!

Sharon went shopping downtown but, not surprisingly, couldn't find anything suitable for the wedding, no, the *chasunah*. E-mails began flying. Dina now went on a shopping spree in her hometown and rounded up six possibilities — one for the wedding, the rest for *sheva brachos*. She had her daughter try them on, since she was the same size as Sharon, photographed her and e-mailed the pictures to Sharon. Upon approval, she shipped the six outfits cross-country.

Dina knew that six dresses do not make a *chasunah*. Sharon had never before attended a *frum* wedding and didn't know the first thing about an *aufruf, sheva brachos* or anything in between. So Dina guided Sharon every step of the way.

How do I know this story, and where do I fit in? I am Dina's Partner in *Chessed*. I run a network of used clothing *gemach*s, and Dina's community periodically sends us shipments. I was on Dina's e-mail list from the beginning of the planning. If she was coming to Eretz Yisrael, she wanted to visit the packages she sends in their natural habitat, the *Beged Yad L'Yad* clothing *gemach*, and meet me, too.

When she arrived in Israel, I gave Dina a tour of our place on Rechov Rashi where she saw an empty box of hers being used for storage.

"It's a *yom tov* when they come," I tell her, referring to the cartons of clothes Dina and her community send over. "I make a "Grand Opening of the Cartons" Sale in my house and let the women at them; it's part of the fun. Many of our customers assure us that they have virtually eliminated budgeting for clothing because they come away from such sales, or from any visit to the *gemach*, with bagfuls of clothing for just pennies."

I called together all the English-speaking shoppers in the *gemach* at that time to tell Dina and her husband, who is a very active partner with moral support (and babysitting when she's out preparing the next shipment), about how everyone benefits from and appreciates the *gemach*. Small world—Dina met a woman from where she grew up who used to baby-sit for her best friends! The woman did a rave job on showcasing the *gemach*, and Dina went back home fortified with new impetus to keep on going. And more dresses for the *chasunah*.

On the day of the wedding, someone asked Dina, "So where do you fit in? Are you the aunt, the neighbor or what?"

She was thoughtful for a moment, and then replied, "I'm not family; I am much more than that. I'm a Partner."

If you're interested in becoming a Partner in Torah,
please visit www.partnersintorah.org, *call* 800-STUDY-4-2,
or email info@partnersintorah.org.

DISENGAGING

ROCHIE AND THE PHONE *Number*

BY CHAVI CHAMISH

*I*n August of 2005, the settlers of Gush Katif were forced out of their homes. Over the following weeks, their settlements were bulldozed and the land given to the Arabs of Gaza. The displaced families set up tent-cities or were distributed to hotels around the country.

A week later, a young woman named Rochie called me from New York.

"I have your number from the three Chabad boys you met in Ofakim. They said you're volunteering with the Gush Katif families in one of the hotels. After hearing some of your experiences, I decided I had to do something. I'm going to collect donations. I want to come next week. Can you arrange for me to help out in your hotel?"

Rochie's words, tumbling out with such earnestness, took me by surprise.

I had met the three Chabad boys two weeks earlier when thousands of Gush Katif supporters had gathered in the town of Ofakim. It was the last attempt to break through the army barricade and join the sealed-off settlers before the destruction of the Gush. The Chabad teenagers had approached my older son and asked if we had room to take them in our car.

"We arrived this morning from the States to show our support. We couldn't handle sitting in New York doing nothing."

"That's an extraordinary thing to do," I said. "People here feel very alone in the struggle, as though the world is indifferent. So thank you. And about the car ... we have one space. Take my mobile number. If you can't find someone to take all three of you, call me and one can come with us."

A while later, the boys phoned to say they had a lift.

At about 2 a.m., everyone was divided into groups and allocated guides with army maps that they would use to bypass the main roads. For the next four hours, we bounced along dusty fields and back roads, sometimes getting the signal to extinguish headlights as we silently passed near army and police checkpoints. It was a very crazy night, given that it was *our* army, *our* policemen. A handful of the thousands got through to Gush Katif, but not us.

At sunrise, I'd had enough of the adventure—the bouncing and dust and landing up in clumps of trees. We turned in the direction of home, the car, our faces, as well as our dog, completely covered in yellowy-brown dust. As we emerged from the car outside our apartment block, several neighbors on their way to *shul* stared in astonishment.

Later in the day, I recalled the three young Americans. I decided to phone and see how they had fared. Like my sons, they were feeling pretty down, questioning why they had come. They were very touched that I'd called.

Little did I know what ramifications that one brief call would have. A few days later, after the destruction of the settlements, the three Chabad boys called to say good-bye and again said thanks for caring. They were returning to the States. By then, I had started volunteering with the displaced families in the Caesar Hotel and told the Chabad boys some of the tragic stories. I related how I had turned up at the Caesar to see how I could help, just when the first busload of displaced people arrived. In the lobby, an exhausted middle-aged woman stood at the reception desk angry and sobbing, with two white supermarket bags, her only belongings, resting against her feet. "What did we do wrong? Twenty-three years ago, Shimon Peres himself approached my husband and *begged* him to move to Gush Katif to be the Rav. What did we do? What crime did we commit, to be dragged out of our home like lowly criminals?"

I listened in silence. I had no words.

I also related how another family arrived in their own car. The parents took their six young children up to the hotel room. When the father went back to get their belongings from the car, *everything* had been stolen, including his entire electronic equipment worth thousands of dollars, necessary for his business. On top of the trauma and exhaustion, the family now had no change of clothes, diapers, toothbrushes, nothing. The following day, the father learned that because of a technicality in the insurance policy, he was not covered. The stories of suffering and indignity were endless.

On returning to the States, the three boys described the experiences to their friends and family. One of them was Rochie, the one who then called me.

A week later, I picked her up at the airport. She was in her early twenties, sweet and modest. She brought suitcases full of toys and toiletries together with thousands of dollars. She also brought the exact electronic equipment that had been stolen from the car.

The next morning, we took the equipment to the young father. He couldn't speak. He stood in the lobby, touching his hand to his heart, again and again, tears running down his face.

Through a cousin, I arranged for Rochie to move into the Hyatt where, together with other volunteers, she worked constantly with the families, bringing sunshine to everyone she met. Often, she would take the children out for the whole day to give the parents time to collect their thoughts, organize their lives. The families couldn't get over the fact that Rochie had come all the way to be there for them.

Rochie gave the donations she had brought to the settlers' Rav. Shockingly, the settlers still had to pay the mortgages on their bulldozed homes.

In the confusion of the forced evacuation, some had not grabbed their documents though they had prepared them, or had lost their bags during their resistance to being forced onto the buses, and so had no access to their bank accounts. Endless problems.

Several weeks later, Rochie had to return to the States for her studies. She wheeled her suitcase along the hall early in the morning. As she went, door after door opened up, the grateful families coming out and clapping, the children hugging her, everyone wanting to give one last show of *hakaras hatov* to this young woman who had entered their hearts and lives in such a real way.

I often think of those three young men and how they had felt their efforts had been for nothing. Not only had their coming touched everyone whom they met, but through hearing about their experiences, Rochie had come, with her extraordinary contribution.

Once back in the States, she did not stop. She organized the production of a documentary film using the video footage she had taken while in Israel. The film, called *Courage to Survive*, was shown in the States, South Africa and Canada, generating thousands of dollars of donations at fund-raising evenings.

I was privileged to have met four special young people, each one of them with a designated mission, each one with a Jewish soul that is the true inheritance of the Jewish people.

MY NEIGHBOR from BOMBAY

BY SHIFRA SHOMRON

Several days ago, in her sixty-square-meter *caravilla*, Simcha Shimshon passed away. Simcha used to be my neighbor. Back in beautiful Neve Dekalim, she lived only three houses away.

I never knew much about her life story. She was from Bombay, India, and had only one child, a grown son who lived with his family in the adjoining agricultural community of Gadid. Simcha loved her only son, daughter-in-law and grandchildren. She constantly kept pictures of them before her.

I had often seen her slowly shuffle to a neighbor's house in order to sit in their comfortable living room or lively kitchen and watch the children play and tease each other, or listen to the grown-ups' conversation. In her own house, Simcha always kept herself busy, but I am sure that the elderly lady from Bombay found it much more interesting and enjoyable to sit in her Yemenite neighbors' house and follow their family dynamics.

You see, Simcha loved life and, in her limited way, tried to be a part of ours and our neighbors' lives.

There were times in which I would walk over (reluctantly, I shamefully admit) and help her around her house: I would sweep her floor, adjust the living room blinds, change the bedding and dump the garbage. She always greeted me with a smile, shuffled around and followed my actions. When I finished, she would present me with a toffee candy or two.

My mother would encourage all of us children to spend time with our elderly neighbor, but, except for my three youngest siblings, none of us children really did so. Simcha's attempts to sit in our living room didn't work out despite my mother's willingness since the rest of us were not comfortable with this breach in our privacy.

Yet, Simcha was happy. And busy. During the week, she would sit in her Yemenite neighbors' house, watch the children merrily playing at the playground right across the street, do arts and crafts at the Golden Age Center in Neve Dekalim, and attend Hebrew *ulpan* classes at the bomb shelter next door to her house. For Shabbos and holidays, she always went to her son's house and visited her grandchildren. She had her own house on a quarter of a dunam. She was independent, active and alert.

But Prime Minister Sharon's "Disengagement Plan" changed things.

Like all other Gush Katif residents, Simcha also was banished from her house. Her devoted son managed to procure a *caravilla* for her in the Nitzan *caravilla* site. Since she was from Neve Dekalim, she was placed in the Neve Dekalim section.

Simcha was very sad. She didn't like her new situation. She didn't know where her old neighbors were (most of them being scattered in hotels), she didn't have anything with which to occupy herself, the bus driver whom she knew and liked and who used to drive her to the Golden Age Center back in Neve Dekalim was now unemployed like most former Gush Katif residents and she yearned to return to her house in the Gush.

Seeking to improve his mother's situation, her son arranged for her to move to a *caravilla* in the Gadid section; in fact, to live right next door to him. So, yet again, Simcha's belongings were packed up and moved. It must have been very stressful for her.

Monday, 22 Elul (September 26, 2005), Simcha had either fallen and hit her head or had suffered from a stroke. Death was practically instantaneous.

Such was Simcha's demise. The last thing she had been doing before her death was sitting on her couch and flipping through a picture album of her grandchildren. Former Gush Katif residents came to Nitzan from the various hotels to escort Simcha to her final resting place and comfort the grieving family.

I'm sorry that I never knew more about Simcha. Not even her exact age is known (she was in her mid-eighties); they didn't have such documents in Bombay. She was clearly a well-educated woman, fluent in both her Indian dialect and the English language. Looking at her fine facial features and at how she carried herself, my mother would say that she must have been very beautiful when she was younger.

Oh, Simcha! Happiness seems to have forsaken us for a time, but we will meet again! May your memory be blessed.

LEGACY

Coming to
AMERICA

BY MIRIAM SHIELDS

*E*astern Parkway, Utica Avenue, President Street — these names seemed strangely familiar. Driving through Crown Heights several weeks ago, my memory stirred as I wove together fragments of stories heard from my father about his mother's arrival in America.

The year was 1928. My grandmother's ship docked in Hoboken, New Jersey. She had come alone from a small town in Poland, leaving behind elderly parents and a younger brother serving in the Polish army. She was a tall, sturdily built woman, whose physical strength masked her profound loneliness. Thirty-one and still unmarried, she had experienced years of disappointment searching for a suitable mate. She hoped that in America, her fate would change. Among her meager belongings were two pairs of oversized silver candlesticks — the family heirlooms that were her most precious possessions.

My grandmother was met at the dock by a close relative who brought her to his home in the Bronx where she had intended to live. Within hours, the family sat down to a bountiful dinner consisting of meat and other delicacies. Still overwhelmed by her new surroundings, my grandmother looked around at the food spread out on the table. Pointing to a dish of butter amongst the meat items, in violation of the Torah commandment forbidding eating milk and meat together, she hesitantly asked her relative's wife, "What is this?" Attempting to reassure her, the woman answered in Yiddish, "It's butter .... Forget about Europe, my dear. This is America."

That night, my grandmother slept fitfully, distressed and uncertain about what to do. Could she live in a home where Jewish laws were disregarded? How could she compromise the values with which she had been raised? She longed for her parents, whose wholehearted devotion to Torah had shaped her life. Years before, her father had come alone to America with the intention of settling and eventually bringing the family there. Deeply pained upon witnessing the widespread desecration of Shabbat, he decided to return to Europe permanently.

She envisioned her mother, who hours before my grandmother's departure had carefully packed the oversized silver candlesticks, entrusting them to her. She knew that she must hold on to the beautiful Torah traditions against all odds, despite the necessity of immigrating to a place fraught with challenge.

Early the next morning, my grandmother reached a decision. She took a slip of paper with an address written on it: 286 Utica Avenue. She rode on a rattling train from the Bronx to Brooklyn, clutching the slip of paper, apprehensive yet determined. Finally, she arrived at the home of an aunt and uncle, immigrants for many years. Could it be that their lifestyle had not been affected by their American surroundings? Here my grandmother recognized the signs for which she had been searching. A large wooden *mezuzah* was affixed to the front doorpost. The familiar aroma of freshly baked *challah* wafted from the modest kitchen. "Please join us for Shabbat," her aunt offered.

My grandmother eventually became a permanent member of her aunt's household. After three years, a potential match was suggested to her, a learned Russian immigrant known for his upstanding character. My grandmother agreed to meet him. Their first meeting took place on a Friday night. The man was as enthralled with the oversized silver candlesticks glowing in that Crown Heights home that Shabbat as he was with his future wife. My grandparents were married shortly after their first meeting.

My grandmother lived until the age of ninety-three. Today, her oversized silver candlesticks stand on the top shelf of my parents' dining room bookcase. I will treasure them for the rest of my life. My grandmother's heirlooms. Her most precious possessions.

ALL
We Take WITH US

BY BRACHA GOETZ

*H*ere comes a tale of what happened to us,
When we left Eretz Yisrael.
We sent back a lift with all of our stuff.
Big deal. That's a story to tell?

Well, the part that is worth telling
Is we'd lived there for over ten years,
Becoming observant, redirecting our lives.
We returned here with many fears.

How could we ever manage to keep our values straight?
Would Torah start slipping behind?
And then our lift came. We opened it up.
What we were looking for, we did find.

Nearly all our possessions, all of our things,
Had been stolen from us. All our stuff.
The uninsured crates had been broken into.
"Leaving Home wasn't enough?!"

We realized later, we'd needed this *potch*,
Given with complete love, though we'd cried.
The message it brought didn't hit right away.
Only after the pain could subside.

You see there was just one box left untouched,
One crate in which no thieves had pried.
Can you guess what was in that one heavy box?
All our Torah books were packed inside.

That one box was all that remained.
The symbolism was not lost.
This experience left an indelible mark,
At comparatively little cost.

That's really all we can take with us.
In the other boxes we'll find … nil.
Just the Torah box goes from one world to the next.
So which need we work hardest to fill?

How could we ever manage to keep our values straight?
What would save us from slipping back yet?
The invaluable lift we were hoping for came.
What we need is precisely what we get.

Blessings of the

GREAT-GREATS

BY MICHELLE GORDON

We are five generations of firstborn daughters, and I am in the middle. Just back from Israel, I am showing photos of my newborn *sabra* granddaughter to my Russian-born grandmother in her apartment in Maryland. "I want to hold her!" Bubbie pronounces. Bubbie Clara's ninety-six years have not erased her memories of the fragrant scent of a baby's head, tiny puffs and sighs, tickly scratches of little fingernails. "I want to hold her!"

Eleven months later, Bubbie got her wish. She was snoozing on her couch as we crept into her tiny apartment. She wasn't expecting us until morning, but we came straight from the airport, not wanting to delay the meeting any longer. Bubbie looked up, focusing on us in the dim twilight. She scrunched up her features in intense emotion as we lowered eleven-month-old Bracha Tehilla onto the sofa beside her.

The baby, like her mom, was exhausted from the long journey from Israel, but was wide-eyed as she met her great-great-grandmother for the first time. In these dreamlike, birthing-room-intimate moments, we were enveloped in a warm cocoon of maternal bonds.

Like a biblical listing of begats, we were: Clara from Berdichev, who begat Barbara from Manhattan, who begat Michelle from Brooklyn, who begat Sarah from Maryland, who begat Bracha Tehilla from Jerusalem. Time seemed to slow down and contract as the life spans of five generations converged and intertwined around one another.

For months, Bubbie had been trying to get the genealogy straight: "My little Michelle is a grandma; I must be ancient!" Now, Bubbie Clara's years seemed to melt away as her tender brown eyes peered into two wide-open blueberries.

"Jeepers, creepers, where'd you get those peepers," Bubbie crooned while Brachala's pudgy hands patted her Bubbie's bushy, unruly eyebrows and her wispy silver hair. "You're not dreaming; I'm really here," Bracha's gestures seemed to say.

The little blond *sabra* with the eight-toothed smile charmed and disarmed, already having mastered the coquettish head tilt to get attention. Certainly, she had no trouble getting the attention of Bubbie Clara, who has a Ph.D. in *kvelling*. Watching my grandmother kissing the *hentelach* and *feeselach* (hands and feet) of my granddaughter, I had the strange sensation of seeing myself as a baby in my grandmother's arms.

Bubbie, always the dancer, pushed Bracha's stroller while doing the conga step down the hall. And Bracha, on the verge of taking her first steps, pulled herself up on Bubbie's walker. They gazed at each other in wonderment and delight from opposite sides of the walker, from opposite ends of their lives, from opposite ends of the unbroken chain.

THE
VELVET *Tablecloth*

BY SHAYNA HUNT

For most children of Holocaust survivors, the lack of extended family connections and even the lack of family information is an agonizing common factor. As the daughter of a child survivor, I am not immune to the deep-seated pain of having very little extended family.

My mother was three years old when her family managed to escape France by being smuggled into Switzerland during the Holocaust. Some years after the war, when my mother was ten, she and her immediate family emigrated from Belgium to America, leaving behind a small group of extended relatives who eventually scattered themselves to Canada and Australia. Only a very few remained in Belgium.

Sadly, the Holocaust emotionally affected my mother's immediate family so severely that they were not close while she grew up. By the time I was born, I had very little connection to the few aunts, uncles and cousins that I did have in America.

When my husband and I were making a party for our first daughter's bat mitzvah, it pained me that only three guests (outside of my husband and our three daughters) were actually my family members. Whereas it's true that I am blessed with many friends, the little girl inside me was crying out for family connections. I needed something that I had never had, and the pain and resentment of that void caused me tremendous anguish.

Searching for strength, I contacted my only known *frum* relative, fellow writer and first cousin once removed, Rosally

Saltsman. Though she lives in Israel, we are fortunate to stay in touch through email, and I am glad to say that our friendship has been such a gift! Through countless emails that were sent back and forth, she transferred to me some much-needed *chizuk*. The result of that immense strength rekindled my passion for Torah and helped me to reach out to the only other extended family I have in Chicago.

I bravely sent an invitation to my mother's brother and his wife. I have to admit that after having virtually no relationship with my aunt, she must have found it strange to be invited to something so out of the blue. I can't even imagine what she must have been thinking when they received the invitation, but I was happily surprised when she replied that they'd be happy to attend.

I think the best result happened after the bat mitzvah celebration. My aunt and uncle live, interestingly enough, in the same area of Chicago that I do. Since they live within walking distance from me, I decided to invite them for a Rosh Hashanah meal, and they accepted. I have to admit that right after they arrived, it was a bit awkward. Not only had we been out of touch since I was a little girl, but I am now religious and it might have taken a little getting used to at first. Nevertheless, by the time we were eating the meal, we were all talking and sharing like old friends—like family. It felt good.

In the middle of the meal, my uncle (who was only seven when the Holocaust began) started to cry in deep, wrenching gulps.

My aunt was horrified and embarrassed. She tried to stop him, but I interrupted her. It felt right to simply say, "We're family, let him cry. I am sure if he's crying this hard, he must need to. Don't be embarrassed!"

So my aunt, my husband, my children and I waited in the silence that was punctuated by my uncle's heartbroken sobs.

"My grandfather," began my uncle as he attempted to dry the tears that cascaded down his face, "was a very special man. He was very religious. I grew up in the apartment complex that my grandfather owned. My mother, my father and I had our own apartment, but we would eat with my grandparents. And I remember Shabbos."

My uncle cried as he told beautiful tales of my great-grandfather and of the holidays and the *Shabbasos* that he remembered as a boy. "My mother and her mother would light the Shabbos *licht* every Friday night. They lit their candles on a dining room table that was covered with a beautiful brocade velvet tablecloth that had been a wedding gift to my mother and father from my father's parents." He halted briefly and then continued sadly. "After the war, we came back to our apartment only to find that our relatives, including my beloved grandfather, had been murdered and our belongings stolen." My uncle paused, and he began to cry again. I wasn't seeing him as a man in his early seventies, but as a young boy whose safe and happy world had been turned into a living nightmare that would haunt him for a lifetime.

"My mother found an aunt who was still alive. Apparently, this aunt had somehow managed to rescue two things from our apartment before everything had been taken, and had given them to my mother—a mantelpiece clock wrapped in the Shabbos tablecloth. When I got married, my parents gave them both to me. They are precious antiques that represent what we had before the war murdered and destroyed our family. I had always thought I would give them to one of my children. But my oldest son is married to a Catholic girl, and I wouldn't dare give it to them because they wouldn't understand what that tablecloth means. My other son is not religious, and he wouldn't appreciate the sentimental value."

My uncle paused a moment as he looked pointedly to my

husband and me. Then he tapped my table that was decorated with my best *Shabbosdik* finery. "This," my uncle said, "is the table where the tablecloth belongs. Here, it will see Shabbos again!"

I received the tablecloth the following Erev Yom Kippur. When I placed it on my table, my children along with my husband and I stood running our hands across its rich, plush surface. We thought of the relatives who had once touched it. I thought of Rosally. It was her grandparents who had given my grandparents this tablecloth as a wedding gift. It bonded Rosally and me together on a deeper level. I felt as if I had come home. As I ran my hand across its surface, I connected with my relatives who knew the meaning of being Torah Jews. I was finally touching something that they had touched.

My oldest daughter was the first to speak as we silently absorbed the tablecloth's "energy." With her hands placed reverently on the middle of the tablecloth, she said, "I think it was right here that our great-grandmothers kindled their *licht*."

I am humbled to say that the velvet tablecloth resides peacefully in my home, anticipating the next Shabbos. My family and I had been given a gift—a peaceful embrace from generations long ago that seemed to cry out approvingly, "On here, we will see Shabbos again."

THE
SWAN

BY TOVA RHOEM

I loved that crystal swan. It had been a wedding present from my Bubby. Bubby understood me and loved me unconditionally as only a grandmother can.

I remember the day she gave me the swan. It was three short weeks before my wedding. I was a bundle of nerves and excitement. She called me on the phone and asked if I could stop by her house for a short while. I really did not have time, but I managed to squeeze it in between a gown fitting and a shopping trip for furniture. I walked into her house somewhat breathless. She was waiting for me with a fresh plate of cookies.

"Oh, Bubby, I can't eat these; I just came from a gown fitting!" I laughed as she pushed the plate closer to me. She knew me too well. Those cookies were my favorite. I took one. She smiled at me and said, "There's always room for Bubby's cookies, even inside your wedding gown."

"I hope so!" I replied. Then her face turned serious. "Rachel, I bought you a gift. It's something that comes with all of my love and heartfelt wishes for you. Let it accompany you into your new life." She then took out a large box wrapped in silver and white paper. I carefully unwrapped it and opened the box. I gasped. Sitting inside the box was a large crystal swan—delicate and beautiful.

"Oh, Bubby, you shouldn't have. I don't need a gift to know how much you love me!" Her answer to my comment has remained with me until today: "I know that. But I want this swan to remind you of even more than how much I love you. Look at the swan; see that no matter what, the swan holds its neck high. It always looks graceful and elegant, and never loses its composure, even when things are tough. Rachela, married life is not always easy. No matter what, always hold your head high and rise to the challenges that will inevitably be part of your life. And remember that it's worth it. Every struggle is worth it, for, like the swan, there is nothing more beautiful than married life."

All the weeks of nervous excitement seemed to cave in on me as I hugged Bubby and cried. Her words have remained with me since then, though she passed away only ten years after my wedding.

The swan had an important place in my new life. To me, it represented all the hopes, dreams and excitement of my *kallah* stage of life. Those idealistic wishes can be easily lost in the sea of married life, but the swan helped me hold onto them. Whenever things were hard, I would look at the graceful swan, holding its head high, and I almost heard my Bubby encouraging me. It gave me the strength to straighten my shoulders and continue through life.

Then it happened.

I had been married sixteen years and was the proud mother of eight children. My fifth child, Sima, was six years old at the time. She was a creative girl with a vivid imagination. I never knew where her antics would lead me. She was named after my bubby, and in many ways I saw similarities between them. On the day that it happened, I came home from work exhausted. The baby had not slept the night before, and all I wanted was a nice, comfortable bed.

The scene that met my eyes when I walked through the door seemed to be straight from my worst nightmare. Sima sat on the couch, crying, surrounded by several of her siblings. A few feet away from her were shards of crystal. In my head I prayed that it was just a broken goblet, but in my heart I knew what it was. My swan. I gasped involuntarily. Sima looked up, saw me and began crying harder.

All my children knew how much Bubby's swan meant to me. I begged myself to remain in control as I carefully asked, "What happened?" Sima's tear-filled eyes looked up at me as she shakily replied: "In school we learned the story of the Ugly Duckling who really was a swan. I was just trying to act it out and I picked up the crystal swan for a second and it was heavier than I thought and ... and ..." Here she ran out of words and began crying again.

I slowly sat down on the couch next to her. My mind was racing. "What would Bubby want me to do now?" Her swan had been my reminder to always keep my head up and never lose my composure. It had been my reminder of Bubby's love. To me, it had represented a kind of continuity of Bubby, even after her death. And now it was gone.

I looked at my Sima, named after Bubby, and suddenly the realization hit me. "Is there any greater continuity of my Bubby than my own daughter, my own flesh and blood, especially one who is named after Bubby? Is there any greater sign of the love between Bubby and me than the fact that my daughter carries her name? Is there any greater *zechus* (merit) I can give Bubby than to raise this child properly and bring Bubby *nachas* in the *Olam Haemes* (World of Truth)?"

I took a deep breath and leaned over to hug Sima. "Don't cry, sweetie. Mommy's not upset. It's only a swan made of crystal. We have each other, and that's more important." Sima stopped crying and looked up at me with her clear blue eyes that are so much like Bubby's. "I love you, Mommy."

"I love you, too, sweetie," I replied as I went to clean up the shards of crystal. The swan was gone, but the lesson would stay with me forever. I think Bubby would have been proud.

COOKIES
for LIFE

BY TOVA YOUNGER

World War II had been going on already for four long years, four years during which I entered adolescence, four years during which I tried to understand all that was happening in my small town of Riskava, located on the border of Romania and Hungary. Four years of rumors, restrictions, fears and prayers.

Then came the day we had been dreading; we were all forced to leave our homes and live in the ghetto. Our stay there lasted one month; a month filled with anxiety, apprehension and many prayers.

Too soon, it was our turn. My family was given 24-hour notice to evacuate the ghetto and go to a destination unknown.

My mother, may she rest in peace, epitomized the role of a Jewish mother. As she packed, she worried about all of us, especially about me. I was the youngest and had been ill frequently. I was also thin and caught colds easily. What would be with me? She decided to make a quantity of cookies—rich cookies, with a good amount of oil and eggs, something to give energy, that wouldn't spoil, and that I, her fussy daughter, would eat. She packed warm clothing and whatever food she could, preparing until the last minute. The next morning, it was time to leave the ghetto.

We were loaded onto cattle cars, in horrible conditions, but at least we were together. I asked my mother for some cookies, but was only given one or two. "We have to dole them out frugally," my mother explained. "We need them for wherever they are taking us."

Finally, we arrived and were rushed outside. The Germans told us to leave our belongings, assuring us we could retrieve them later. We stood there for a few moments in confusion, awaiting instructions. Suddenly, my mother turned to me. "The cookies! Let me at least go and get the cookies that I baked for you. Wait here, I am going to get them. I'll be right back."

She hurried off. We did not embrace or say good-bye, for she was coming right back.

"Forward!" screamed the German soldier. "Why are you all waiting? March!"

Perhaps she returned, but I was no longer there, having been moved along with the group of young people. That night, separated from her, I cried for her … and for my cookies. Too soon, I realized that my dear mother was gone. I would never see her again. My grief for my mother was too deep to cry out for, but as days turned into weeks, and food was disgusting and sparse, I continued to moan for my cookies.

Finally, another girl kindly said to me, "Don't cry about your cookies. Even if you had gotten them, how long could they have lasted you? A few days? A week? A month? All that time has passed already; had you gotten your cookies, they would have been long gone. Forget about them."

I realized she was right, but I continued to think about them. It was only after the war was over, as I relived my memories, that it dawned on me. Those cookies had saved my life! Had my mother not disappeared, I would have clung to her and joined her in death in the crematorium. Hashem had other plans for me and took her away at this crucial point, preventing me from rushing to my death. My mother wished to nourish me with those cookies … and she did.

TROUSSEAU

BY ADAM ELIYAHU AND
DEVORA GILA BERKOWITZ

We're neighbors, Naftali and I, but we have little in common. He's already married off two children, while my eldest is not quite in first grade. He's a high-profile heavy-hitter, an aggressive businessman, and I'm a misanthropic hermit, happy to be left alone. But we do share two passions—a good cup of coffee and even more, a good story.

Naftali's son, an old friend of mine, owns a cafe that brews the best espresso in Israel. So, after a long night at work, I decided to treat myself—or let him treat me with his usual offer of a free cup of coffee. Naftali happened to be there and waved to me from the corner where he sat out of the way watching the waiters lift wooden chairs onto the tables as they prepared to tuck in the restaurant for the night.

"So what's the young man doing these days?" he said in his amusing, lilting manner.

"A little fund-raising for a worthy cause," I said simply. He smiled so wide I could see the dimples peeking through his graying beard. This was a sure sign that I had given him an opening for one of his celebrated tales. Settling back into my chair, I sipped the last drops of my espresso, knowing that I was in for a good one.

Naftali licked the whipped cream off his mustache, stroked his beard with one hand and began. "When I was in yeshiva, I had a problem with arrogance. My rabbi knew that the best way to break my pride was to send me out to collect charity, door-to-door. The cause was the best. A young couple, both orphans, was getting married. But he knew that it wouldn't be enough for me just to ask for money. He wanted me to get some real-life experience, something that would strengthen my connection with Torah.

"So he sent me and my friend to the richest neighborhood, notoriously anti-religious. With our *peyos* and beards, *kippah*s and knee-length *tzitzit*, we walked the street lined with luxury sedans feeling as out of place as honey-dipped *challah* at the Pesach Seder. The first door we knocked on was quickly slammed in our faces. At the second, a man peeked through the eyehole and asked us to wait for a minute. A moment later, he opened the door and yelled, "Get 'em!" We heard the sound of claws clicking and sliding across marble as a Rotweiler ran right toward us. For out-of-shape yeshiva *bachurim*, we made amazing time getting out of there.

"The next three hours were a repeat of the same scenario, over and over again. They threw insults at us, shouted names I cannot repeat, even spat in our faces. My friend and I were totally disheartened. We vowed that the next door would be our last.

"We knocked and a woman who appeared to be in her fifties opened the door a few inches. Looking over the chain, I noted that her dress was down-to-earth, simple clothing and unpretentious jewelry no doubt purchased at the most exclusive shops.

"'Ye-e-esss?' she chimed, peering down the length of her nose at us.

"I braced myself, saying the words without feeling, glad that one way or the other, our mission was almost at an end. 'Excuse me, madam, but we're collecting for, uh, a young couple who are getting married next week. They are both orphans and, uh, have absolutely nothing.'

"I'll never forget how we stared at each other for a long

minute over the taut chain that kept the door from opening fully. I waited for her to say something, hurl an insult or break into an angry outburst, but she remained silent, her mind wandering far away. Finally, she cleared her throat. 'P-please wait here a moment,' she said, removing the chain. The door opened as she retreated into her luxury apartment. My friend and I shot glances at each other, ready to make another run for it. We were relieved when the lady came back alone, signaling for us to follow her into the kitchen.

"'Would you like a cup of tea?' she asked softly, her voice becoming warm.

"We hesitated. She sensed our apprehension. Our unspoken reluctance to eat or drink in her non-kosher house hung between us. Without waiting for our explanations or attempts at polite refusal, she poured hot water into two Styrofoam cups.

"'Do you have a car?' she asked.

"I nodded, a bit confused. She disappeared back into the apartment, returning shortly with her arms full of packages. She set them down in piles near the front door; expensive linen sheets from the city's finest stores. She went back and forth, stacking more bags and boxes in the hallway. You should have seen it — everything a new couple could possibly want: costly silverware, beautiful glassware, crystal serving dishes, fine curtains and tablecloths, silver candlesticks — all of the highest quality.

"Then she joined us at the table with her own cup of tea served in an elegant china cup. After her first sip, she put down her tea, the cup rattling slightly against the dish.

"'What took you so long?' she sighed. 'I've been waiting quite a while to give these things to someone. They've been … in the way, taking up space. You see,' she continued, 'my only child — my daughter —'

"She cleared her throat. 'My daughter was engaged to be married three years ago. She was on her way back from the engagement party when her little sports car was hit by a truck. I couldn't bring myself to return all the lovely things I had bought. The money was irrelevant. I felt attached to the gifts and couldn't just get rid of them. Please pass these things on. I'm sure it's what my daughter would have wanted.'

"It took us several trips to load the car, and when we were finished, there wasn't an inch to spare. The older woman stood like a statue, her arms crossed over her chest, and watched us with a sad smile. The elegant packages seemed so out of place in my old junker. I was sure we looked like thieves and prayed we wouldn't get pulled over by a cop. Without receipts for all the merchandise, we would surely have been arrested. As we gathered the last of the packages, she stepped forward and nodded with satisfaction."

Naftali stopped in mid-story. I was eager to know how it all ended.

"Nu?" I nudged him.

"Well," he said, stretching his long legs under the table, his hands clasped behind his head. "As we were about to pull away, she stopped us."

"Yes?"

"'Come back in nine months,' she called after us, 'I know the perfect store for baby clothes.'"

HEROES

PURIM
in the FOREST

BY JON GREEN

My father told me many stories about his years as a partisan fighter in the forests of Byelorus. This one he would tell every Purim:

Purim, 1942. The Naroch forest, Byelorussia.

It was getting close to Purim. Boris started remembering his father's home and how wonderful Purim was every year. They would celebrate Purim in a big way with lots of alcohol, costumes, Purim *shpiels*, good food, the Megillah reading and so on. He would wake from these memories and daydreams in tears, as he realized where he was now and in what circumstances.

Here in the forest the conditions were rough. It was freezing cold, and there was never enough to eat. And you could never risk getting drunk. You had to have your wits about you so that Ivan wouldn't put a bullet in the back of your head or stick a knife in your side when you were unprepared.

Boris stood there shaving, thinking about life as it had been in Disna before the war. Then he remembered his fellow Jews, the ones he had once discovered hiding in a hole in the ground when he was out exploring the forest. He remembered their shrunken, depressed faces, the rags they were wearing and the stench that came from their hole. A thought occurred to him. He was going to celebrate Purim with them! A real Purim in which they would smile again. He was determined to do it.

So he devised a plan, which he shared only with his brother,

Fima, and a couple of other guys from other partisan units. They were going to have a Purim party there in the forest! *But how could you celebrate Purim under such conditions?* he asked himself. Easy, he realized. A little vodka, a good wash, some good food, a fire and no Ivans ... that would do it!

The planning process went on over a number of days, during which time they collected some of the things they needed—firewood, warm clothes for those Jews in the *malina,* sweets, a couple of bottles of vodka. But most important of all was to find someone who could *lein* (chant) the Megillah.

Of course, they had no Megillah in the forest, but there were plenty of Jews amongst the partisans, so one of them must be a Megillah-reader. As the word went out that a Purim gathering was being planned, the excitement grew. The Jews were whispering to each other; the non-Jews suspected something was going on but no one would tell them anything, of course. The tension was palpable. There were fights.

But despite all the excitement, no one came forward to volunteer to recite the Megillah from memory. It was, perhaps, too awesome a task. After all, the Megillah is famous for its great length and its unusual *trope.*

One day, coming back to camp after collecting "taxes" at one of the neighboring villages, Boris had a brainstorm. What about the Jews in the *malina*—those poor hiding scarecrows? Perhaps among them there was someone who knew the Megillah well enough? That night, after his fellow partisans had finally fallen asleep, he sneaked out, bundled up in his fur coat and cap, and carrying his rifle, of course. He headed for the *malina,* hoping that the Purim redemption would be found there.

As he approached, he heard the voices of people arguing. They were quarreling over something or other quite heatedly. They often fought in there. He knocked on the hollow tree trunk, knowing that it was really a disguised chimney. His knocks echoed down the hollow cylinder and suddenly the voices fell silent. After a while, he heard a scratching sound and a little window suddenly opened out of the snow. "Who is it? Who is out there at this hour?" asked a trembling voice in a heavily-accented Russian.

"It's me, Boris — Beryl — Grenimann," came the answer in a good Litvak Yiddish. "Ah, Boris ... Beryl!" came the response and a door opened out of the snow. A thin, withered old hand waved him in.

Boris brought with him the tragic news of the latest liquidations of some more ghettoes in the region. Some of the women wept, others pried him with questions. Had anyone escaped? The children just stared their empty, hollow stares. Then silence reigned again.

He brought out the bread he had hidden under his coat and a flask of oil. (No one asked questions about what kind of oil it was anymore.) The food was devoured in minutes. No comments, just the sound of desperate eating, loud chewing and sighs. Then, finally, a few words of gratitude came his way; they all knew he risked his life bringing them the little he could. More tears. Silence.

Now it was his turn to ask. "Next week, in another five days, it will be Purim. We are looking for someone who knows the Megillah well enough to recite it," he said. "Is there someone like that here?"

They looked at him strangely. "Purim? Purim ... what are you talking about?"

The Jews in the *malina* were from the town of Miyadzel. It was the winter of 1942. Altogether thirty people, mainly women and children, were crowded into the one dugout under that hollow tree. Amongst them were the two daughters of the Rebbe and five of their children.

Boris repeated his question: "Is there someone here who can read the Megillah for us?"

Silence.

A shaky, high-pitched voice came from the dark, crowded corner: "Me. I can do it. I used to read the Megillah in the main synagogue every year. I know most of it by heart. I can do it. I know I can."

Everyone turned to see who was speaking. His eyes had become accustomed to the dark and his pupils had expanded, but Boris could barely make out the face in the corner. He picked up the candle that had been extinguished earlier and relit it. In the flickering light, he saw a tall blond boy with green eyes and a wisp of a beard on his chin. He was smiling. The thought of celebrating Purim had already put a smile on his face. *What a fine young man*, thought Boris.

"What's your name, boy?" asked the partisan visitor. "What are you called?"

"Mottel, sir," came the answer. "My name is Mottel. My grandfather was the Rebbe of Miyadzel. He taught me the Megillah."

The boy's mother then spoke up. "Mottel, are you crazy? These are not normal times. It is dangerous. We will be discovered. They will murder us all, as they have so many already. Who can imagine celebrating Purim this year? Better we just stay hidden here until the troubles end," she said.

"No, mother," answered the boy. "I will do it. It is a *kiddush Hashem* to do it. The Rebbe would have wanted it, I'm sure."

"All right," responded Boris, "we will be back to discuss details, but for now, Mottel, start practicing. We will try to procure a Megillah somehow, but if we don't, we will rely on your memory. Good night to all of you. Be strong!"

And Boris left.

Days passed. They huddled together in their *malina*. It was bitterly cold. Mottel sat on his own in the corner reciting what he remembered of the *Megillah*. Sometimes he asked his mother or sisters if they remembered a word. He fought with them over the candlelight. He wrote down some of what he remembered on scraps of paper that he managed to salvage. It was bitterly cold that winter, and he shivered as he struggled to protect those pieces of paper from the ever dwindling little fire.

Boris returned. He asked to speak to Mottel. "Mottel," he said, "tomorrow is Purim. Are you ready?"

"Yes," Mottel answered sadly. "I can manage about half of the Megillah from memory."

"Okay," came the response. "Then we will go ahead with our Purim plan." He turned to the others in the *malina*. "Tomorrow, you must all be ready to go just after dark. We have a surprise prepared for you." Then Boris left.

Mottel's mother, Chava, was worried. She mumbled to herself at night. Her eyes were red from crying. Everyone could read the fear in her face. Her advice to her son was clear. "Don't do it, don't go!" Mottel, of course, was adamant, too. He must do it. So he continued to practice.

Meanwhile, Boris and his friends had completed their preparations. They had chosen a clearing in the forest where a couple of hundred Jews could gather. They had built some *sukkah*-like structures for shelter around the clearing. In one of those, they had placed the firewood. Nearby, dug into the ground and carefully camouflaged, they had placed the drinks, food and sweets that they had managed to "organize" from surrounding villages. A couple of partisan guards regularly patrolled nearby to keep an eye on things. Stealing was very much part of the partisan way of life; it was a matter of survival.

Boris had met with a peasant in one of the nearby villages. A supporter of the communist underground, he had often helped in the past. But this time the request was an unusual one. Boris had told him that he wanted to arrange for hot water baths for some thirty Jews who were in hiding in the forest nearby, and who had not been able to wash for months. Could Ishtvan help him do this? The peasant thought for a while and then said he would help organize this. Boris explained to him that it was a Jewish holy day and that being clean for the occasion was a religious obligation.

The next day, toward evening, Boris, accompanied by three of his toughest comrades, came to collect the Jews to take them to Ishtvan's farm for a wash and some new clothes. The Jews were beside themselves with joy at the thought of leaving the *malina* after so long and being clean in honor of Purim.

They marched through the snowy forest toward the nearby village, accompanied by the four partisans. Mottel and his mother continued to argue about the Megillah-reading, while the others, now and then, nervously hushed them.

"Mottel, Mottel," she said, "we have lost so much, so many. We are all that remain of the town of Miyadzel. How can you agree to endanger all of us by agreeing to this foolishness?" The last strands of her once brown hair had turned gray over the past couple of weeks, and the deep lines across her forehead seemed to have become even deeper.

"*Sha!*" called out one of the partisans suddenly in Yiddish. "You must all be quiet now. We are approaching the village. There might be Germans here."

But there were no Germans. In fact, all they met as they walked into the little village were more partisans patrolling the outskirts. "This is a liberated village," said one of them to the newly arrived guests. "Liberated by night, but still controlled by the Germans during the day. They patrol here every day, but they don't have the courage to hang out here at night anymore." His face, lit by the full moon, glowed beautifully. It was gaunt and unshaven, and he was not smiling, but his two dark Jewish eyes twinkled at them as they passed him.

What a scene met them at Ishtvan's house when they finally arrived. Laughter and cries of delight as one by one all the poor Jews were washed and supplied with new clothes. Boris noticed how thin and white their bodies were, but he said nothing. Everyone was given a little swig of Vodka, too, which really warmed their insides. Ishtvan's family seemed to enjoy their defiance of the Germans, and all were there to lend a hand in one way or another. Mottel noticed how pleased the farmer's oldest son was as he kept emptying and refilling the two little tubs with hot water. It was he who offered the vodka around afterwards. His powerful, muscular arms turned gentle as he handed Mottel a little vodka to drink. He looked at him directly, his eyes smiling. "Peter," he said, pointing to himself, offering him his ruddy and rough hand in a friendly gesture. "Mottel" came the reply as he shook his hand. Mottel managed a smile, and then turned his attention to the vodka in his other hand, which he finished greedily after making the appropriate blessing.

When it came time to go, Peter escorted them to the edge of the forest. Mottel walked silently beside him. Mottel wondered what had led this *goy* to be so helpful and friendly to them. Would he have taken such a risk to help him if the situation were reversed? He doubted they would ever meet again, but he felt he would like to somehow repay him his kindness. They waved as the little group of Jews and their partisan escorts re-entered the forest.

The march back into the forest was much more relaxed than the walk there. Everyone was smiling. Even Chava, Mottel's mother, no longer argued. Someone started up a Yiddish *liddel*;

others joined in, only to be silenced by their partisan escorts who warned them not to make so much noise.

They approached the clearing in the forest where a campfire burned brightly, and men and a few women dressed in old fur coats, some wrapped in blankets, sat huddled around the fire trying to warm themselves. They were singing Yiddish songs and talking quietly.

But the Megillah reading with the partisans was not to be. A tall, mustached partisan (obviously an officer) came riding up on a horse and glowered at them. "That's Colonel Markov," someone whispered. He ordered them to disperse immediately before they attracted German attention. No one argued with him. Within minutes, the fire was put out and the partisans disappeared, as if into thin air.

The Miyadzel Jews made their way to their old hiding place, the *malina*. No one spoke, but the disappointment could be felt in the air and could be seen in all the sad eyes around the little room. Then Mottel spoke up. His posture and the flash in his eyes spoke determination. "It is Purim, friends," he reminded them. "It's a mitzvah to hear the Megillah. Let me recite it to you." They agreed, and he started to tell the old story of Esther and Haman, Mordechai and Achashvarosh, as Jews had done for so long in so many places. Suddenly, they heard a knock on the chimney. Silently and frozen with fear, they opened the window to find Boris and his brother, Fima, standing there. "We have come to hear the Megillah," they explained, smiling.

A few days later, Boris came by with food again; what they had brought "home" from the Purim party was already gone, though the good memories of the peasant's home lingered on. He brought very sad news. Apparently, the Germans turned up at Ishtvan's house the next morning. Someone had informed on him that he was cooperating with the partisans. His eldest son,

Peter, had been led out in front of the house and shot before the eyes of his family. Stunned, Mottel turned to his mother and said sadly, tears in his eyes: "Mother, you were right. We should have stayed here."

My father, "Boris," would tell me this story every year, his eyes filled with mischief and pride as he remembered their daring and how they had outwitted the Germans. Only the bitter ending, telling me of Peter's execution the next morning, was left out all those years. When I told him I was planning to write down some of his partisan stories to share with others, and mentioned the Purim wash story in particular, there was a long pause on the phone. He then added the terrible postscript. The sting and shock of that small addition cut through my soul like a knife. What had always been an innocent anecdote with a happy ending about Jewish resistance during the war was wrenched out of my insides and reconnected with the horror that I knew the Nazi times had been.

A7855

BY DANNY BROTHERS

*L*istening to my iPod, I boarded the #18 bus headed for the city center. It was a sticky, hot day in the middle of a Jerusalem summer; the sky was clear of clouds, and I dodged the sun by jumping from bus stop to bus steps. Any summer day in Jerusalem is too hot to be caught under the intense glare of the moon's better half, and I was glad to grab a seat on the air-conditioned green Egged.

My designer backpack was a bit too heavy, holding many of my frivolous electronics, so I eased myself next to an amiable looking old lady instead of moving further down the rows. She was probably around seventy-five, a short, typically forgettable old lady wearing a light blue cardigan over a ribbed white shirt. She was clutching a couple of grocery bags. That was about all I noticed. I was quite preoccupied with rushing to meet a friend on Ben Yehuda Street, and the woman was just another old woman.

Because I had a large backpack, as soon as a roomier seat became available, I moved over so I could spread out. The seat was directly across the aisle from my previous spot. Looking out the window, mouthing the lyrics to a sad tune, I lost myself to the passing landscape. I was deep in thought, believing that I truly was the only person on earth, besides my waiting friend, of course. I rested my leg on the backward-facing seat in front of me as the song I was singing just reached the climax. A deep bass drum contrasted by a smooth, rising piano line, a voice breaking out in a desperate plea for clarity, a plea that echoed what I had demanded from the world for many years. I was relaxed and content in the moment.

"*Slee-cha, slee-cha* ... (Excuse me ...)" The old lady who had been trying to get my attention finally succeeded. Who knows how long she had been trying. Following her polite interruptions, she threw a quick Hebrew statement at me, which of course I understood none of. But from her gesticulation I knew what she had asked. "Get your feet off the seat that other people are going to use, young man."

Like many self-centered, absent-minded and arrogant young men, I was more than annoyed at this reprimand. *Who cares if I rest my legs on a raggedy seat?* I responded with a nod, however, and removed my feet, but I also threw in a shrug of the shoulders and a muttering of English.

An interrupted song has no credibility. Seeking a new artist, I attempted to find whatever dream it was that I had before, but I found over the next minute or so that I could not regain my previous contentment. I despise it in myself, but I am quite sensitive to any type of admonition. Avoiding the glare of the sun through the tinted window, I looked back at the lady to get a better picture of her face. Ever since I began lifeguarding years ago, I have had a staring problem. And in Israel, where the standard nighttime activity is people-watching, I have very little compunction about this habit. What I saw when I took a second look at the seemingly boring old lady horrified me, and any sense of being victimized was cast aside.

A7855. Clear as day and black as night, there it was. Her number: A7855. This was her name to the Nazis. And only seconds before I felt contempt for her, just as the ugliest monsters had years before. A7855 was her tattoo identification number.

How could I not have noticed when I sat down next to her? I had noticed that she was carrying groceries—milk, eggs, bread and apples. I recorded those items in my memory, but I was blind to the tattoo, just as her simple request was mangled by my own self-perception and blind conceit.

I could not take my eyes off her number. I apologized to Hashem. She looked so normal. This woman, A7855, was simply riding down the road from the market, a far cry from what she must have experienced during the Holocaust. The Holocaust. How far away from my own dreams was that horrific event? But not for her; she knew that place and time intimately.

What could she have been thinking when I brushed off her rebuke so childishly?

The bus slowed to a stop, the brakes pulling the passengers forward and then quickly snapping us back and forward again. The survivor stepped down the steps through the open double doors at the middle of the bus, and slowly walked out of view. I watched her every second of the way, amazed that we have made it to this land—heroes like her, along with impertinent children like me.

LALA

BY ORLY AISH

*T*here are no pictures or any other documents about my Aunt Lala and her short life.

Everything was destroyed. The family was deported, and when my dad returned, there was nothing left. This is a child with no photos, no grave, who only existed vaguely in the memory of one person — my dad, her brother.

I only heard about Lala when I was a mother of three. No one ever talked about her, and even her name was forgotten. My dad, her brother, remembered only her nickname: Lala.

When I told my dad I wanted to write a memorial for her, and I needed to know what she was like and how she looked, the only thing he told me (it was too painful for him to even talk about her) was that she was thirteen when she died and was beautiful with a long blond braid. With only this information, I reconstructed her character.

When I let my dad read the finished story, he cried and said I could not have done a better job depicting Lala. This was my reward.

At eighty-one, my dad is the only survivor of his family still alive. I made a vow to tell the story of Lala to as many people as I can.

On a stormy night, I saw Lala in my dream. It was the first time I saw her. She had my father's features, with narrow lips and a sharp nose. She had my grandmother's hands, with wrinkled skin, a crooked middle finger and the rough fingernails of a hard-working woman. (It *was* a dream, after all.) Her hair was blond and shiny, in a thick braid down to her waist, and her eyes were glowing. In my dream, Lala was thirteen. She walked erect, her shoulders wide. Her eyes were joyful, and on her lips I saw the shy smile one often sees on the lips of girls turning into women.

A few days before Lala appeared in my dream, my grandmother, Dvora, her body wrapped in a shroud, had been laid to rest. Heavy rain flooded the cemetery. Family members who came to say farewell said they did not remember such a harsh winter. We stood crouched under the heavy rain, watching the hole in the ground filling with soft mud. Wet and shivering, we held tight to the umbrellas that the wind threatened to snatch from our hands.

Before she passed away, at eighty-six, my grandmother lay unconscious for eight days in the hospital. It was there, at my dying grandmother's bedside, that I first heard the name "Lala."

Dvora put another old wool blanket full of lice on the feverish Lala. In Transnistria, Ukraine, the winter of 1941 was the harshest in forty years. Dozens of typhoid sick Jews lay side by side in an abandoned old shack, which used to be a pigsty of a local village. Wooden boards divided the pigpen into small spaces. Straw covered the frozen ground, and the bitter cold penetrated the shattered tinted glass in the high windows. Seven days earlier, Dvora had arrived there with fifteen-year-old Israel and thirteen-year-old Lala. A week before they arrived in the crowded pen, the family had been deported from its comfortable home in Loboka. On short notice, all the Jews were ordered to pack a few of their belongings and gather in the village square. From there, they were driven in open carriages to the pigpen. Before the deportation, Dvora was wise enough to pack some of her dead husband's clothes to sell, one by one, for some food.

Lala first started showing signs of typhoid the day they arrived. Stomach cramps tortured her young body. She had diarrhea and high fever, refusing to put anything in her mouth. For the last two days, she was feverish and did not respond to her mother's touch or voice. She mumbled meaningless sounds, shaking her head, her face and hair wet with sweat. Two hours earlier, Dvora had sent her son, Israel, yet again, to the nearby village with an old pair of men's shoes to exchange for some food. She was sitting at her dying daughter's side, completely detached from the moans and groans of the other sick people around her and holding a piece of cloth, soaked with water, on her child's forehead. She thought that soon her son would return with a little corn flour, from which she could make thin porridge, or with a small piece of bread, which she could soak in water and crumble into her daughter's mouth.

The memories and smells of the Sabbath delicacies she used to cook in her big, comfortable house filled Dvora's mind. She remembered how she used to light the big stove with chunks of wood brought from the nearby city, and how every Shabbos the stove was covered with big, steamy pots. She could still smell the sweet aroma of the slow-cooking foods that her family loved so much. Boiling chicken soup with onions, potatoes and carrots, fresh from her garden, bubbled in the big pot, to which Dvora added fat bones of a turkey neck to enrich its taste. In a small pot, she cooked corn flour for a sweet corn pie, while three loaves of *challah,* browning in the big oven, filled the house with the irresistible smell of fresh pastry.

The sound of the footsteps of her son, Israel, returning from the village tore the sweet comforting memories from Dvora's mind. He took five small potatoes and half a loaf of bread out of his pockets and sank on the ground, exhausted from hunger and from the long journey. Dvora immediately rose to her feet. She scooped out some of the soft part of the bread with her fingers, soaked it in the water tin and went to Lala. With one hand, she opened her sick child's mouth, and with the other, she rolled the bread between her fingers to soften it and put it in her mouth. Lala did not respond, and the soft bread, mixed with saliva, leaked from both sides of her mouth. Dvora sighed in despair. She knew her daughter was doomed. During their seven-day stay in the crowded pigpen, eighteen people had died and were buried in the mass grave a hundred meters away. Dvora painfully remembered that only a few months earlier, her beautiful, healthy, blooming, thirteen-year-old daughter used to spend hours each day writing poetry. How she loved to sit on her wide bed, covered with a white lace bedspread, and write. When she completed a poem, she hurried to the kitchen and read it to her mother, her voice full of excitement.

The next day, under the setting sun and in the bitter cold, two men laid Lala's tortured body in the big mass grave and covered it.

The curtain around my grandmother's hospital bed was still spread shortly after her death. Behind me, my father and his aunt were talking about Lala. My father said they should commemorate her on my grandmother's gravestone, and his aunt sighed sadly and asked what name they would engrave. Both were silent. They could not remember her given name, only her nickname. I felt a shiver run down my spine. A girl was born and lived in this world for thirteen years. A horrible disease ended her young life, her body was thrown into a mass grave in a foreign land, amidst a dark war ... and no one remembered her name.

"Lala." The sound is so soft and loving. *Lalka* means "doll" in Polish, so she must have been the sweetest baby girl and the nickname lingered as she grew up. For a brief moment, I saw the faces of my three children and a feeling of agony and of a great loss weakened my knees. What did she look like? There is no picture. Everything was destroyed in the inferno of the war.

On the thirtieth day after my grandmother's death, the clouds scattered and a warm sun caressed the family members who came to the cemetery. When we stood around the marble gravestone, I put my hand on the words engraved in the stone:

"In memory of Lala, a pure soul,
who perished in the Holocaust when she was only thirteen."

I made a vow to tell the story of the girl whose name was forgotten.

Adi's ANGEL

BY SARA YOHEVED RIGLER

A di Huja, a sixteen-year-old Jewish girl, observed the second anniversary of the terrorist bombing that almost took her life at Hadassah Hospital, preparing to undergo her twenty-sixth operation. On that fateful Saturday night two years ago, Adi and her girlfriends had gone to eat ice cream sundaes at a café on Jerusalem's Ben Yehuda pedestrian mall. Two Arab homicide bombers blew themselves up, killing twelve young people and injuring scores more.

The doctors told Adi's mother, Mollie, that they couldn't save her daughter. When, despite their predictions, Adi didn't die, the doctors told Mollie that they would have to amputate her right leg, which was partly torn off by the bomb. But, miraculously, they were able to reattach the leg. Two years later, however, it has still not healed, leaving Adi with constant infections and pain. The threat of amputation hangs relentlessly over her.

I am sitting beside Adi's bed in a drab room in Hadassah Hospital, a week after her latest operation. "What did they do this time?" I ask Adi's mother.

"They put in a metal plate and a pin," Mollie answers.

"But she had a metal plate in her leg all last winter," I protest. "I remember her telling me how cold it made her feel. And the last operation was to take out the plate because the doctors thought it was causing her infections."

"Right," Mollie nods. "But her leg is broken, so they had to put the plate back in."

I look at this petite girl sitting in the bed and ask, "So how do you feel, Adi?"

Adi answers with a single word: "*Mar* [bitter]."

What can I say to console her — for all the pain, for all the trauma and for two years gouged out of her young life? I am struggling for something positive to say when my attention is drawn to a commotion at the door of Adi's ward. A man is trying to maneuver a wheelchair past chairs and beds. Sitting in the wheelchair is a young woman with a pretty face and two shriveled legs. The man pushes the wheelchair right up to Adi's bed.

"I came to say good-bye," the young woman says to Adi. "I'm being discharged."

The young woman's name is Leora. She and Adi converse for several minutes in Hebrew too fast for me to follow. Then they lovingly bid each other farewell. Leora's father backs the wheelchair out of the room.

"What's with Leora?" I ask Adi.

"She's totally crippled," replies Adi. "She's paralyzed from the waist down … from birth."

Although I never philosophize with terror victims, my relationship with Adi is close enough that I venture: "You know, you can see your cup as half empty or half full. Compared to Leora, you're very fortunate. When you recover from this operation, you'll walk again."

"I'll hop with a crutch," Adi corrects me resentfully.

I try another tack. "You've lost a lot, Adi, but you've gained even more. Most girls your age are shallow and self-centered. Because of all you've suffered, you've become deep, compassionate and sensitive to other people's suffering. Before the terrorist attack, could you have related to Leora so warmly?"

Adi thinks about this. "No," she replies, shaking her head. "I wouldn't have related to her at all. I wouldn't want to look at a crippled girl. I wouldn't talk to her."

"See how much you've grown?"

Adi is not listening to me. She's gazing past me at the hospital corridor. Suddenly, she shouts, "It's Malkiel! Mommy, go get him! Bring him in!"

Mollie runs out to the corridor and returns with a man in his mid-thirties wearing a *kippah* and dressed in the blue uniform of municipal sanitation workers. "Malkiel, I'm so glad to see you!" Adi effuses, smiling broadly.

I gaze at this man. I think I recognize him, but why is he dressed like a garbage collector? "You're Malkiel Lerner, aren't you?" I ask.

I had met Malkiel at a wedding last May. At that time, he had given me his card that read: "Brother of the Wounded." He explained that he has made it his mission to visit every wounded person in Israel—whether from a terrorist attack or an army-related incident.

He had shown my husband and me a photo from his own wedding two years before. In the photo, Malkiel, the heavyset bridegroom, is sitting in a chair being hoisted into the air. "That's Ohaad," Malkiel had pointed proudly to one of the young men lifting his chair. "He lost his leg in the war in Lebanon in 1997. But there he is, dancing and lifting my chair."

The day before I met Malkiel, a terrorist attack had occurred in Afula, a two-and-a-half-hour drive north of Jerusalem. Although I usually visit terror victims in Jerusalem hospitals, I was not about to undertake the long drive to Afula, even though I own a car. Malkiel, by contrast, had risen at five that morning, and, lacking a car, had taken a bus to Haifa and from there another bus to Afula to visit the victims. Fifteen hours later, he excused himself early from the wedding to go work his night shift as a hotel clerk. I was in awe of Malkiel's dedication.

But now, in Adi's hospital room, I can make no sense of what I'm seeing. Why is he wearing a garbage collector's uniform? I know that one of his brothers is a lawyer and another is a computer programmer. I ask him why he's dressed like this.

"I lost my job at the hotel," Malkiel answers, "so I'm working as a street cleaner. You can view it in two ways: You can say that it's dirty, disgusting work, or you can say that Jerusalem, the holy city, is the courtyard of the King, and that I'm privileged to make the King's courtyard cleaner and more beautiful."

Talk about seeing the cup as half full!

"Besides," Malkiel continues, "the hours are good. I get up at 4:30 a.m., pray, catch the 5:30 bus and start working at 6:00. I finish by 1:00, so I can spend two or three afternoons a week visiting the wounded."

Since Malkiel keeps up with all the terror victims in Israel, I ask him for an update on twenty-year-old M.J. I had last seen M.J. thirteen months ago in Hadassah's Intensive Care Unit hours after a Jerusalem bus bombing. She had suffered massive injuries to her head and neck; her face was swollen to twice its normal size. A month later, I encountered her parents in the I.C.U. waiting room. M.J. was still unconscious.

"Two weeks ago," Malkiel announces, smiling, "she *bentched gomel*. Do you want to see her picture?"

Malkiel reaches into a plastic bag and pulls out a pile of photos. He hands me one of himself standing next to a sprightly young woman whose smiling face resembles a purple topographic map. I recoil in horror and wonder how any woman, vain as we are, could let her picture be taken like that. I wonder even more at her smile.

"Let me see!" Adi asks. I hand her the photo. Now Malkiel starts to pass around other photos. There's one of Malkiel standing with two smiling young women. One is M.J. The other woman's face has the same grotesque purple terrain as M.J.'s. "This one," he explains, pointing, "was a waitress at that Tel Aviv café that was bombed."

Adi, appalled, asks, "Will their faces heal?"

"M.J. will eventually look better," Malkiel explains, "but the waitress will always be scarred."

Adi grimaces. I say to her, "*Baruch Hashem*, your pretty face wasn't damaged."

"*Baruch Hashem*," Adi responds, still staring at the picture.

"You have a lot to be grateful for," I add. "The truth is, your cup is three-quarters full."

Adi acquiesces with a nod. She looks up at Malkiel and tells him how bitter she has been feeling. Malkiel launches into a story.

"When I was nine years old, I was run over by a car and badly hurt. I was unconscious for a week. I had a major concussion—and my leg was shattered. A lot like you," he adds, looking at Adi. "It took me many years to recover. I never finished school and never got a high school diploma. I was bitter. For nineteen years I would look up at heaven and ask, 'Why me? Why did I have to suffer so much?'

"Then one day, when I was twenty-eight years old, it suddenly came to me in a flash: I had to suffer such injuries so that I could help other people who are injured. I realized that my mission in life is to give strength and encouragement to the wounded. That's when I committed myself to visiting every single wounded person in Israel, no matter where they are."

I glance over at Adi. She is transfixed by Malkiel's story. Her cup is getting fuller by the minute.

Malkiel continues. "When I visit the wounded, I tell them what's written in *Pirkei Avot* (Ethics of the Fathers): 'Who is rich?

The one who is happy with his portion.' I tell them: 'If you have eyes, teeth, hands and feet, rejoice!' To people like Ohaad, who don't have feet, I say, 'If you have eyes, teeth, hands and a head, rejoice!'

"And you want to know something? It really works. They trust me because they know I've gone through something similar. They invite me to their weddings and to their babies' *brissen*. They feel like they have a friend who understands them."

I turn to Adi and ask, "Well, what do you think?"

"I think that Malkiel is great," she responds.

"You could be as great as Malkiel," I tell her earnestly. "Because you've suffered so much, you can also help people who are suffering."

Adi grins. Her cup is full.

Readers who wish to contribute to Malkiel's mission can send donations to:

Malkiel Lerner
P.O.B. 29144
Jerusalem 91291
Israel

MIRACLES

REFLECTIONS:
GUSH KATIF
and Beyond

BY SARA LAYAH SHOMRON

*I*t was a new reality. My beloved Gush Katif was destroyed—beautiful, dynamic communities turned to rubble and their inhabitants banished. My family, along with fifteen hundred other Gush Katif families, were rendered homeless, many of us jobless and in a daze from former Prime Minister Sharon's unilateral withdrawal from the Gaza Strip, his Disengagement plan, August 2005. A population that withstood Arab terror and attacks—mortar and rocket attacks, roadside shootings and ambushes—was disarmed and cruelly torn from its beloved land.

My dream had become a nightmare. But like all bad dreams, we wake up to a beautiful new day filled with opportunity and promise. I told my children, "With Hashem's help, we'll take our positive energies and put them to good use elsewhere in Eretz Yisrael."

My husband and I wanted to live our lives where we could make a difference and be active participants in our unfolding Jewish destiny. We visited a number of religious communities in Yehuda, Shomron and Galilee in search of a community we could help strengthen with our brood of seven children. It brought back memories to me of when my husband and I initially made *aliyah* as newlyweds looking for that special community. We came to realize that our identity and sense of being is tied to Gush

Katif. We decided we would help rebuild the community of Neve Dekalim in Nitzan.

Here at Nitzan, it's marvelous to freely ride my bike to the sea, walk with the children and dogs through the nature reserve and have no fear (so far) of bombs or being shot at on the road or at home. However, during my first time at the sea, I heard shooting from a nearby army base, but I figured that was so we'd feel comfortable. More recently, rockets have targeted Ashkelon, with one landing about ten minutes away from Nitzan. There isn't a single bomb shelter at our *caravilla* site, and I shudder to think of the human catastrophe were one, *chas v'shalom*, to reach us. One of my younger children recently asked me why we don't have a "Red Alert" in case of an incoming rocket. I answered it would merely cause panic, as we don't have a bomb shelter for cover. Besides, I further explained, while we don't rely on miracles, these temporary flimsy prefab *caravillas* in which thumbtacks can hold up pictures are a constant reminder that security comes from Hashem; it is Hashem in Whom we put our trust and faith.

My husband, like many here at the Nitzan *caravilla* site, was unemployed for two years. With Hashem's help, one of the former Gush Katif farmers with whom my husband worked rebuilt his agricultural greenhouse and is growing insect-free vegetables. My husband is the *mashgiach*, doing comparable work as in Gush Katif.

As for my children, they are getting on with their lives with a healthy attitude and outlook.

Baruch Hashem, my children are forward-looking and growing into independent young adults walking faithfully and humbly with Hashem, and they are contributing members of this society.

My second daughter, Shifra, authored her debut novel about an Israeli family living in Gush Katif from pre-Intifada II until the Disengagement. Her novel enables anyone, as she frequently writes, to "travel beyond time and beyond location into my Gush Katif."

My three sons have taken advantage of living in an ongoing construction site and have created amazing wood furniture. We're talking Woodwork 101 with a wonderful picnic table, bookshelves, chair and bench.

My son Baruch was in tenth grade at the time of Disengagement. He was a student at the Katif Yeshiva in Gush Katif and had to find another yeshiva, as the Katif Yeshiva didn't re-establish itself. The Jerusalem Nativ Meir Yeshiva, complete with an elementary school, opened its heart to the Gush Katif children, and my son completed his studies there. He went on to study at the advanced Mercaz Harav Yeshiva. He was there during the terrorist attack.

With much thanks to Hashem, he is okay, but we mourn for our dead and pray for our wounded. May Klal Yisrael have the faith, strength and courage to carry on, and may we go forward as the youth whose lives were so cruelly cut short would have.

Baruch told me he would have ordinarily been in the yeshiva library learning at the time of the attack, but he had been hiking that day and had just returned to the yeshiva. He went to his fourth-floor room to download his photos. In fact, just moments before the attack, he had emailed some photos to his sister Shifra.

Suddenly, as Baruch tells it, he heard what sounded like firecrackers. Since it was the new month of Adar, he thought nothing of it but then recognized gunshots. He quickly hid under his bed and prayed. He heard pandemonium, screams, gunshots. He thought he was one of the last remaining in the yeshiva. Later he would tell me that he felt like he was inside a house on fire and there was nothing he could do to help himself. He loathed feeling so helpless and refused to be a victim. With unbelievable clarity of mind, he decided to get out of the building by way of the balcony. Baruch continued praying and then climbed over the balcony, dangling there. The distance between the fourth and third floor balcony is considerable, so he couldn't reach the third floor balcony. A man standing on the third floor who saw what Baruch was trying to do raised his arms and instructed my son to put his feet into his uplifted palms. Baruch did so and let go of his balcony. With Hashem's guidance and help, my son made it safely to the ground and made a run for it with the other man following.

Once across the street, Baruch phoned me from someone else's cell phone. I had no idea there had been an attack. My brain listened, but I couldn't quite register what he was telling me; that would come several hours later when I broke down in uncontrollable tears. Having left his cell phone in his room, Baruch had the presence of mind to phone me. Had he not, and had I learned of the terror attack and called his cell phone, I would have gone crazy listening to the unanswered ring.

Three students from my son's study group were murdered, as were five other students, and many were injured. May Hashem avenge their deaths, and may their families and all of Klal Yisrael be comforted among the mourners of Zion.

Several months later, as I walked into the Nitzan *caravilla* site, my temporary home away from home—may Gush Katif be speedily rebuilt—I heard and felt a BOOM! Once in my crowded *caravilla*, I turned on the computer and learned that the earth shaking underfoot was the result of two rockets that had landed at the Ashkelon Hutzot Mall on the health clinic floor, from where I had just returned.

I had just met my sixteen-year-old son at the Hutzot Mall in Ashkelon where he had traveled from his Jerusalem Yeshiva specifically for a 5:15 p.m. medical appointment. He arrived earlier than expected (3:30 p.m.), concerned about traffic on Jerusalem's roads caused by U.S. President George W. Bush's visit. I hadn't expected my son so early and was still at the *caravilla* when he phoned me to inform me of his arrival in Ashkelon. I instructed him to go to the specialist's waiting room area, where hopefully he could be seen earlier, and said I would be there shortly. Fortunately, someone I knew picked me up as I walked toward the highway to catch a bus headed for Ashkelon. As fate would have it, their destination was the same as mine. We got him in to see the specialist, stopped in the pharmacy and were out at the bus stop to catch our respective buses at 5:15 p.m.

Had my son's scheduled appointment time been kept, who knows what …? But *baruch Hashem*, he's safe.

When we share our own personal stories of *Hashgachah pratit*, we are all strengthened and Hashem's name is blessed.

NISSIM

BY JOYCE ROSEMAN

*T*he beautiful hall was crowded, and I wondered if all these people could really be the children and grandchildren of my two nieces! I watched them sing and dance with happy glowing faces, enjoying every moment of yet another family *simchah*. I was overcome with emotion. A saying occurred to me—"Whoever saves one life, it is as if they have saved the whole world"—and I thought of the *neis* that had saved my dear brother-in-law, sister-in-law and little daughter so many years ago. I turned to my niece Rachel, sitting next to me—"It was a *neis*, yes, but really it was many *nissim*," she said and told me the second part of her parents' story.

Her parents' families lived in Hamburg, and by early 1938 the pressure to leave Germany was overwhelming. Naftali Roseman and his lovely wife Betty (nee Gluckstadt) with their small daughter, Henny, took advantage of available work and accommodation in Prague to move to Czechoslovakia, which was a free nation then. It was a unique and ancient city—the pride of Czechoslovakia, with a long Jewish history going back to the eleventh century. The Jewish community took pride in its centuries' old *shuls* and communal buildings and the fact that so many great rabbis and scholars had made it their home.

Naftali and Betty must have felt relief to be out of Germany, but their relief was short-lived. Unknown to them, and to most others also, a secret pact had been made to divide up Czechoslovakia between Germany, Hungary and Poland. In March 1939, Hitler threatened that he would destroy all of Prague from the air unless this pact was implemented. There was no waiting period; the next day, troops marched across the border and occupied the whole of Czechoslovakia.

Naftali's older brother, Herman, had left Germany in March 1933 and gone to England, one of the first few dozen to register as a refugee. There he was able to obtain visas for various countries to enable his family to leave Germany: his sister and her family to England, one brother to South America and Naftali and his family to New Zealand. Although those were sent urgently, he could not have foreseen the fall of Czechoslovakia and the German takeover.

Naftali tried several times to get an exit permit on the strength of his New Zealand visas, but each time he was refused. As the months went by, the situation became more desperate until the only option open to them was to cross the border illegally into Hungary. This was dangerous and costly, as well as frightening, but there was no other alternative. Before setting out, Naftali decided to try one last time for an exit permit. With very little hope, he went to the Permit Office. While waiting in line someone whispered to him, pointing to the German officer they were due to see, "This one is the biggest *rasha*." His expectations sank even lower.

The German officer in charge looked at his passport. Harshly, he said: "You are from Hamburg?"

"Yes."

"Where did you live?"

"I lived in the Grindelstrasse."

"Ha, I lived round the corner …. This Prague is a horrible place."

"Yes, it is a horrible place."

The officer gave him a quick look, picked up his rubber stamp and thumped it on the exit permits—"*Geh schnell, geh schnell* (Go quickly, go quickly)," he whispered.

Naftali needed no second bidding. He ran home, took only a very small case, the train fare and the mere ten marks they were each allowed, and rushed with his family to catch the first train. They traveled through Germany to the coast and were searched thoroughly several times. At one search little Henny was asked, "Where did your mother hide her jewels?" They had nothing, so they were allowed to continue. By the middle of August 1939, they arrived in England, and on September 1 — two weeks later — Germany attacked Poland and World War II began.

Naftali, Betty and Henny stayed in England for several months, waiting for a ship to America. Then again in America, there was another wait for a ship going to New Zealand. At last they were booked to leave and could see the end of their long journey. A few days before sailing, Henny became ill and to their great disappointment they were not able to leave. While waiting for the next sailing opportunity, the terrible news was received that the ship they were scheduled to sail on was torpedoed in the Pacific. There were no survivors.

Naftali, Betty and their daughters, Henny and Rachel, lived in New Zealand for several years before settling in Melbourne, Australia. After the marriages of both Henny and Rachel, the whole family came to Israel, where Naftali and Betty had the *zechus* to see many grandchildren and great-grandchildren. Naftali even merited seeing great-great-grandchildren.

"Bands of the wicked surrounded me; I was confronted by the snares of death. In my distress I called out to Hashem, and to my Lord I cried. Out of His Sanctuary He heard my voice, and my cry before Him reached His ears." (TEHILLIM 18:6-7)

THE ROAD HOME

RAISING A REBBETZIN
– *Listening to the Pintele Yid*

BY ARLENE E. ALYEHS

*M*y story begins in the not-so-distant past of 1984, in San Francisco, California, not exactly a hotbed of Yiddishkeit. My daughter, a bubbly, blue-eyed, blond toddler, had been in a much-acclaimed secular day care known for its careful attention to child development, especially in creative areas like painting and play. She was very happy there and appeared smiling on the day care's newsletter, playing with her best friend, a chubby black boy. The place was the American Dream personified — white, black, Asian children happily, busily learning everything they needed to know to be healthy children, to lay the foundations for future satisfaction in the adult world.

But Hashem apparently had detected that something was missing from this seemingly perfect environment and set about a *tikkun* that surprised me, but ultimately set me on the right path.

In August, my daughter Tamar's day care closed for a month. I was a working mother and had to find alternative child care. I asked everyone I knew, and a newly *ba'alat teshuvah* friend recommended a Chabad family day care.

Having been raised somewhat traditional, but not halachically observant and certainly not *Chareidi,* I was a bit leery of the prospect of such an extreme change for my daughter, but I did agree to meet the young woman who ran what we in Israel call a *gan* (kindergarten).

Not only was I impressed with this woman who was only

twenty-one years old, I was intrigued by her. She was energetic, enthusiastic and purposeful. At thirty-eight, I still didn't know what I wanted to do when I grew up. I really admired her clear sense of direction. Virtually no one I knew was so sure about where he or she was going in life. That alone made me think my daughter might benefit from this *gan*. And learning about Judaism couldn't hurt, either.

It only took a few days to see how much this new environment agreed with Tamar. She came home glowing, reciting *pesukim*, singing songs and showing me art projects based on the *parshah*, like Sarah's tent and Rivkah's well. On Fridays, she brought home miniature *challos* baked at the *gan*. As happy as she had been at her secular *gan*, she was infinitely happier once some Yiddishkeit came into her life.

As a single mother, I took very seriously anything that was good for my child. I simply marveled at how "extra" happy she was. I decided I'd better find out more about whatever magic they were working at the *gan*, so I began to study the *parshah* with the young *rebbetzin*.

Academic study was always my forte, but in Judaic study you need heart, soul and brain working together. I was especially stubborn about the laws of Shabbat; they just didn't make sense to me.

"Why don't you come to us for a Shabbat? There's no use arguing every point. You have to experience it," the young Chabad *rebbetzin* suggested.

It took exactly one Shabbat for me to absorb the beauty and peace of this special day and to realize that there was much more to it than any book could teach. I made keeping Shabbat a goal, even though I wasn't yet ready to commit to steady observance.

Unfortunately, at that time, my daughter and I moved away

from San Francisco to the East Coast for greater family support. Essentially, we traded Yiddishkeit for grandparents. The grandparents were a definite plus, but the trade was not entirely satisfactory.

For a short while, we lived in an apartment close enough to walk to *shul*, albeit a conservative congregation. We stopped eating *treif* meat and, in effect, became vegetarians in order to begin to conform to the laws of *kashrut*.

On some Friday nights, my mother cooked supermarket kosher chickens in throwaway aluminum pans, and we used glass dishes or paper plates and our own set of silverware. At least it was a start.

My parents apparently thought that I was "going through a phase," as I had already been a hippie, dressed in secondhand clothing, visited communes and did many things they thought were not normal, though so many of my generation had done those things as well.

My mother enjoyed lighting candles on Friday night, and both of my parents grew fond of the Havdalah ceremony, ushering in a new week with a final glass of sanctified wine, the fragrance of spices to keep the beauty of Shabbat with us just a little longer and the flame of the braided candle giving us light and warmth until next week's day of rest and peace. I felt as if we were in some small way reconnecting my father to the positive aspects of his boyhood and introducing my mother to a non-demanding ceremony that could bring her precious moments of joy.

In the spring of that first year back East, Tamar's *gannenet* invited us to visit her family in Crown Heights. She was visiting for Pesach, and we shared a memorable Chol Hamoed meal just two blocks from 770, the Lubavitcher headquarters. At the meal, similar to a Pesach Seder, the children were plied with questions to keep them on their toes and awake, and quiz them on their

Jewish learning. To everyone's surprise, Tamar answered a question correctly.

Because she was still quite young, having just turned four, and they knew she came from a nonobservant background, they were so astonished that several of the adults said, "Maybe she'll grow up to be a *rebbetzin*."

That remark got me thinking and made it even more important to me to give my daughter the right education. She started a Hebrew Day School kindergarten. She loved it, and there began to learn Hebrew from an Israeli teacher and to study Chumash.

When first grade was about to begin, my parents, whom we were living with at the time, strongly suggested that I economize on the cost of a private Jewish school and avail myself of the excellent suburban elementary school where I had gone as a child. I caved in because finances were so tight.

As usual, my daughter adjusted well. But then came Xmas with a small nod to Chanukah. The school, despite the official policy of separation between church and state, was swathed in tinsel and pine boughs, but only had a small obligatory bulletin board with cutouts of a menorah, candles, a *dreidel* and the words "Happy Chanukah."

Tamar came home upset. "Mommy, what's all this Xmas stuff? I don't want it! I want to go back to my old school!"

It was the voice of a child speaking with the voice of the *pintele Yid*. I remember thinking that my child is wiser than I am; she knows what is truly good for her.

I declared that I would somehow find a way to send Tamar back to the Hebrew Day School, and that was that. I managed with the help of scholarships and the determination that I would do everything possible to give this child what she knew was rightfully hers.

Next on my list was getting us to Israel where Hebrew would

not be a "subject" but a natural fact of everyday life, where the *chaggim* would fill the synagogues and the streets with fellow Jews and where we would get that extra boost from our external environment while we caught up.

By the time we arrived in Israel in 1991, increasingly, Israelis wanted to be like Americans. When we came to the Absorption Center, the Education and Cultural Counselor suggested that my daughter try the *Tali (Masorati)* stream of education.

"Is it Orthodox?" asked Tamar.

"Well, no, but ..."

"I don't want it."

"Once again, my eight-year-old knew what was good for her. Tamar went on to get an Orthodox education, studied Tanach for a B.A. and a masters degree and married an idealistic young man who became a rabbi. She now runs a women's learning center and has three healthy, happy, little children. My grandchildren. My daughter. My son-in-law, the *Rav*.

The Chabadnikim were right. She did grow up to be a *rebbetzin*, but even more important, she grew up to be a wonderful loving wife, mother and daughter, a lover of Hashem and Torah, and she continues to fulfill the true potential of that bubbly, blue-eyed, blond baby. (Even if you can't see her hair!)

AT THE KOTEL
– Voices of Doves

BY ELLEN W. KAPLAN

*D*oves and sunshine, a melody of prayers, a chorus of gentle voices. The sounds drape me, cover my hair and lift me up in the sweet music of Jewish faith.

These are my recollections of my first encounter with the Kotel, at a time when I knew nothing at all of its history and significance. I had no knowledge — at least no conscious knowledge. And yet, when I touched the stones and heard the prayers, my heart melted and my soul was lifted. Perhaps it was made all the more powerful by my innocence; I had nothing to guard against, no preconceptions to shape my response. My heart was open and something deep within me shifted, opened, *heard*.

This morning, I did what I do each day now: I studied a few lines of this week's *parshah*. *Parshas Terumah* gives instructions for building the Tabernacle, listing the materials we must use. These include precious metals, rare hides, colored stones, and acacia wood. The images in this passage made a strong impression on me, and in my imagination the stones and wood shimmered with light. Then the recollection of my first experience at the Kotel came to mind, and the profound feelings of that time returned.

I have always had a deep affinity for stone and wood, earth's natural materials that resonate with me. Since I was a child, I've collected pretty bits and shards of things like pinecones, sharp pieces of bone and delicate shells from the shore, but above all, stones. It is their steadfast solidity that draws me. I love the way stones hold heat from the sun, warming your hands when you cradle them in summer, or how they keep the cold and chill you when they've been in the shade.

Certain places built of stone have a certain sense of stillness. When I was younger, I believed those places were "sacred," although I couldn't have articulated quite what I meant. What I felt, though, was that in the silence of these places, I could hear Hashem's voice. This was long before I came to know myself as a Jew, but looking back, I believe that this was how Hashem was trying to wake me up to myself, and to Him.

I've been blessed to visit many extraordinary places; I am most attuned to those places made of stone or by the sea that evoke a sense of spiritual grandeur. They seem to wake something in me, and I never fail to be moved.

Some of these experiences have been fleeting, while others have made more enduring impressions on me. In the Jewish cemetery in Prague, I watched autumn leaves falling, and I felt compelled to sit down among the gravestones. In the tiny patch of ground that is the Jewish cemetery of Prague, Jews have been buried for hundreds of years.

The graves are close, and the stones are at all angles. As I watched the leaves fall, I had a comforting sense of being welcomed, that when I was ready, when it was time, I would fall like the leaves, and I would be embraced with love by this community of spirits — that these old Jewish souls would be there when the time came to welcome me home. I felt jubilant; it was in no way sad or macabre, but rather I was bathed in a feeling of deep love and belonging.

During all my travels, I'd never been to Israel. I had no religious training, no knowledge of Judaism, no connection or interest in Israel. However, in 1999, I was invited to direct a play in

Jerusalem, and as my husband had already begun his own journey back toward Judaism, he and I took our first trip to Israel. While we were there, he explored the city while I stayed in the theater and rehearsed our show.

It was with some degree of reluctance that I peeled myself away from the rehearsal room to take an informal tour of the Old City with our hosts from the theater. The day was oppressively hot, and I was impatient to return to the cool basement on Mt. Scopus where we had been working constantly. The charms of the Old City softened the edges of my irritation, and I soon was beguiled by the crush of people, the rushing crowds in the *shuk*, the pushy shopkeepers, the winding streets, the ancient buildings, the press of history and the sacred memories echoing through the Jewish Quarter.

My mood had transformed, changing from impatience through polite interest to deep fascination and sheer delight. I was eager now to see the Kotel, though I didn't know anything at all about what it was. I vaguely knew about a "Wailing Wall" in Jerusalem, but nothing else.

I don't recall much about entering the plaza, but I do remember my husband saying that he was going to *daven* and that I should meet up with him in twenty minutes or so, indicating the top of a wide set of steps. Then someone put a folded piece of paper and pencil into my palm. It was Jessica, an actress with our troupe; I had no idea what she thought I would do with these things. I tried to ask her, but she was gone.

Then I saw. Sunlit, grand, dazzling. As I walked across the plaza, I felt something yielding and softening within me. An old woman handed me a scarf, and I covered my hair. Someone must have handed me a *siddur*, too, because I had one when I approached the wall. And then I was there, standing, touching the stone, pressing my cheek against it. I kissed it, and I began to cry.

Most vivid, now, is my recollection of the stone in front of me, as I touched it, felt its sandy texture, its cracks and crevices, its smoothness in places, and its warmth. Gradually, I became aware of the sounds, the murmurings, the song of doves flying above. I floated up with these voices and the sweet warbling of doves. It was a long time before I realized that what I was hearing were the prayers of the women standing near me. Their prayers were my prayers. And the other prayers, written on scraps of papers, folded hopefully into the crannies in the stone, were my prayers as well. Now I understood why I'd been given paper and pencil, though I felt no need to write.

The serenity fanned by a gentle breeze, the fragrance of flowers, the melody of prayer, all these sensations combined to create a sense of joyous awe. I felt Hashem's presence, and I asked for His guidance. A healing came into my heart, and my road now is much less rough. At the Kotel, unbidden and unexpected, I heard the sweetest music, that of sacred Jewish voices, lifted up and echoing through time by these ancient, sunlit stones.

NACHAS *from* *the* TZURIS

BY ESTHER SENDER

*T*he whole eight-hour journey (including stopover time) was worth it, just for the ten-minute scene I saw on the bus. Although it wasn't what one might call the optimum situation, it was what *nachas* is made of.

First, a flashback to almost two months ago when I was walking back from Shaare Zedek Hospital up some steps to catch a bus on Herzl Boulevard. Behind me on the long staircase was a woman in her forties in slacks, her hair not covered, who quickly caught up. As we climbed the steps at an even pace, we got to talking. Sometime during the conversation, she asked if I needed to travel on Herzl. Before I had a chance to answer, she said, "Don't go on Herzl tomorrow; it's going to be closed off."

"Oy vey!" I exclaimed. "I did need to go on Herzl. But now, after what you told me, I won't." I thanked her and added, "The truth is that now that I won't be going anywhere, I'll clean the house. At least, if I can't go anywhere, I should have a nice clean house!"

She smiled and agreed. "You know what I call that?" she asked. "What?"

"Whenever something good comes out of a bad situation, I always tell my husband, 'That's *nachas* from the *tzuris.*'" She repeated the phrase, lovingly, *"Nachas* from the *tzuris."* She then went on to give me another example of what she meant and repeated it, with new emphasis, to make sure I caught it, *"Nachas* from the *tzuris."*

What pleasure this woman had in saying that Yiddish phrase! And what pleasure *I* got sensing her need, her yearning, to attach in any way she knew to everything those *Yiddishe* words represent. This woman may not keep the *mitzvos* in the fullest of ways, I thought, but she hasn't lost her yearning. If this is bringing *me* so much *nachas*, how much *nachas* is it bringing Hakadosh Baruch Hu?

We have to travel toward Tel Aviv, about an hour ride with traffic. The bus is packed, except for three lone back seats perched on a semi-platform, with a great view of the entire bus. As we make our way back there, it troubles me that almost all the other passengers seem non-religious.

The beginning of the ride is sweet, calm and uneventful. I had forgotten what countryside scenes of Eretz Yisrael can do for the heart.

Back to the scene on the bus.

I look around a little at the "new generation Israeli," wondering what makes them tick. *These certainly aren't anything like the bunches that filled the buses twenty-five years ago,* I think.

I watch as a boy of maybe fifteen or sixteen, his hair a little spiky, fumbles though his knapsack. He takes out a bag, unzips it, takes out another bag, unzips it, and then, shockingly, takes out a pair of *tefillin* and starts to wrap the strap around his arm.

I do a little double take, pinch myself ... it's for real!

He takes out a little black *yarmulke* about the size of a drain plug, puts it on his head, and then positions the *tefillin* on his head.

But before I get a chance to become too emotional, two rows away, a man goes over to the boy with the *tefillin*. I watch in glorious shock as the man borrows the boy's *tefillin* and *yarmulke* and goes through the same motions. The man passes back the *tefillin*, but before the boy puts them away, a soldier from the other end of the back row goes over, taps him on the shoulder and asks if *he* could use the *tefillin*, along with the *yarmulke*.

"*Ya-a-a-a-y!*" I want to shout. "Go, Klal Yisrael! That's the way!"

People all over the world are looking for their morning highs at Starbucks, and *we're* energizing with *tefillin*. What a moment of *nachas*, real *nachas*, for Klal Yisrael.

Then I think, *How can you call this* nachas*? Wouldn't real* nachas *be for them to be putting on tefillin in shul, and not on a bus?*

That was when that woman's words kicked in—the woman from the stairway near Shaare Zedek. This *is* "*nachas* from the *tzuris.*"

This is what that woman on the steps must have meant; maybe this is what Hakadosh Baruch Hu feels.

Lately, my husband has been talking a lot about a massive silent *teshuvah* movement going on around us in Israel, but I never expected to see it this clearly. Here are the signs of changes in trend—and not taking place on the way to Jerusalem, but on the way to Tel Aviv.

Maybe that's why *teshuvah* is so precious to Hakadosh Baruch Hu—because *teshuvah* is "*nachas* from the *tzuris.*"

To SHAKE and to Be SHAKEN

BY RABBI YOSEF WOLICKI

When I was a young rabbi serving a small congregation in Connecticut, I witnessed an event of enormous spiritual significance. It was Chol Hamoed Sukkot. Two members of my congregation who owned a men's clothing store asked me to do them a favor. Would I please stop by their store every morning of Chol Hamoed with my *lulav* and *etrog* so that they could fulfill the mitzvah of the *arba minim*? When I came into the store, I was ushered into the back room. Each brother in turn came into the back, put on a hat, took the *lulav* and *etrog* and said the *brachah*.

The brothers had a Jewish employee who never came to *shul*. They turned to him and said: "How about you?" He hesitated for a moment and said: "All right." He put on a hat and took the *arba minim* in his hands, and then instead of shaking the *lulav*, he himself began to shake. The *lulav* was shaking him! His whole body shook, and he burst into tears. He said that he hadn't held a *lulav* in his hands since he was a young boy. Suddenly, when he took the *lulav* and *etrog* into his hands, he remembered being in *shul* with his father and grandfather. The experience overwhelmed him. This was the beginning of his return to the synagogue and Judaism.

When I walked into that store, I thought that I was helping two men fulfill a mitzvah. Little did I know that the outcome of my bringing a *lulav* to that store would be to awaken a man from a deep spiritual sleep. Perhaps, Hashem also wanted a young rabbi to experience the latent power of the *mitzvot*—the wondrous effect that a single mitzvah can have upon a Jewish soul.

A DONKEY
in MANHATTAN

BY SARAH SHAPIRO

We were sitting next to each other on the #2 bus and started talking. It emerged in conversation that Batsheva worked as a tutor at one of the *ba'al teshuvah* women's seminaries.

Did she have time to tutor me?, I asked. She seemed a little taken aback—after all, we were both grandmothers already. But yes, she said, she'd be happy to.

"What would you like to learn?" she asked.

"Chumash with Rashi," I answered. From the ground up.

She was suggesting various ways to approach this when something occurred to me: "Could we just learn *Balak*?" I interrupted.

"You mean, just that one *parshah*?"

I nodded. In any case, that alone would take me forever. Or longer.

"Fine," she replied, "no problem." After a few moments she said, "Do you mind telling me, though—I'm just curious—why *Balak*? Any special reason?"

"Well," I began. "Once upon a time ..."

It was the end of summer, and the whole world was new. In Connecticut, the dogwood trees slumbered. Daisies and dandelions nodded in the grass. Clouds drifted sweetly across a tender blue sea.

My sister's birthday party was tonight. She'd been on the planet for twenty-four years — just a few more than I — but twenty-four sounded ominous. She was getting right up there into the outer edges of lower middle-age, which meant that I, too, should have turned into an adult by now, with a job and a roommate. I was still just a child, though, invisible and shy. An unknowing child, in spite of my high heels.

I took the train into Manhattan and called her from Grand Central Station. No answer. I dialed again.

Where was she?

There in the dark, old, wooden phone booth, I sat there wondering, listening to the phone ringing in her apartment. Then I tried again. What to do? The family was meeting for the birthday at eight — seven hours from now. I had come in early hoping for some time alone with her before the party.

Walking along through the echoing, shadowy dimness of high-ceilinged Grand Central toward the exits, my heels made a quick, loud *clickity-click* on the cool marble floors, as if I were a real person. I pushed through a dark door, emerging into the sudden muggy brightness of 42nd Street.

Honking, speeding taxis and cars darting in and out of traffic. Big roaring buses. A million people hurrying everywhere. And gray concrete skyscrapers towering up into a hidden sky.

The dense, leaden air hung down thickly over everything, trapping the city under a dirty overturned cup of heat, and the sidewalk was a rushing river of humanity. I started meandering slowly against the flow, upstream. All different colors. A thousand different worlds streaming past, this way and that.

At 43rd, I crossed Fifth Avenue and found myself on the flowery, shady pathways alongside the New York Public Library. Where should I go? The question seemed to be darkening and expanding, until it was asking something else altogether. *Where should I go?*

Approaching the wide stone stairway with its two majestic stone lions standing guard in the midday sun, one on either side of the entrance, I paused.

Suddenly, some kind of atonal Eastern music seemed to burst upon the scene; a group of dancing people in lemon-colored Indian saris materialized as if out of nowhere, and right before me on the path — with a bony shaved skull and long silky orange robes — a skinny young man appeared, spinning and swaying, with the round dot of a Hindu painted low on his forehead, eyes ecstatically upturned. Two pale, skinny arms were circling, stretched out long, and his long fingers rattled and tapped and drummed on a tambourine held over his head. Bangles and looped necklaces of tiny stones, pink and green and blue, twinkling and sparkling. Tiny bells sewn all along his saffron hem. His sad mouth was emitting some moaning chant to an arrhythmic beat.

I stood there, struck dumb by the sight, for even I, who had searched and never found ... searched and searched without knowing what I was searching for ... could spot a pitiful, lost child when I saw one, and a nameless terror took hold of me. I was repulsed, to the core. Inside the Indian costume, inside the shaved head and the ecstatic eyes, I knew all too well that here before me was an American kid in flight from something in Kansas, or Cleveland, or Chicago, a boy on his way to something I didn't want to know about, prancing and dancing madly on thin air.

It was at that moment that a thought went through my mind that had never gone through my mind before, in all my short life. Vividly and distinctly, as if the words were uttered aloud, I thought: *I wish I believed in something.*

Then I turned and went looking for a phone booth.

At 43rd and Sixth, I pulled shut the glass door and dialed my sister again. No answer. My heart sank. Then my mother, back home in Connecticut. No answer there, either. Where *was* everybody?

My sister's number again. Then my father's office. His secretary said he was in a meeting and to call back in an hour.

The sun was glaring at me through the glass. I tried my sister again and *yippee!* The line was busy! I kept dialing.

It was too hot in there. Out of the corner of my eye, I saw that someone was waiting for the phone. The person tapped insistently now on the door, and I was about to say, "Please stop it! This is an important call!" when I found myself looking at a tiny little olive-skinned man in a meticulous black suit and a white beard and a black hat. Black aggressive eyes full of brightness and darkness. Something obscurely familiar about him.

"*Nu?*" he was saying. What did that mean? I'd heard it somewhere. He made some odd questioning gesture of impatience. I pushed open the door. Something about him I didn't like, and something else, that caught my attention. To my own slight surprise, I said abruptly: "You're Jewish, right?"

He gave a quick nod. Those eyes cut me up sharply. He said: "You? Jewish?"

I smiled yes, as if I was doing him a favor.

"What you doing?"

There was no answer to that one.

"*Ach!* Come! You have something to eat!"

I shriveled inwardly with distaste. "No, thank you."

"Come!" He started walking off, very fast. I stood still. He looked back over his shoulder. "Come!" What in the world made me follow? He kept looking at his watch and glancing back at me through the next four blocks to see if I was still there. On 47ᵗʰ Street he darted to the right, and suddenly we were surrounded by people like him.

He went into a big store full of Jews and diamonds, everyone talking. I didn't like it. He scurried up a flight of stairs to a luncheonette and muttered something to the waitress. She looked at me. He sat down.

"Sit!"

I sat.

A slice of pound cake was set down before me. I was on a diet.

"Tea?" he said.

"Coffee." A cup of coffee appeared.

"Nu?" He asked me to tell him about myself. Strange, to be someone's focus like that.

He pointed to the cake. "Eat, eat."

"No, thank you."

"You like it. It's good." He gave me a quizzical look like a knife, with eyes from some ancient place where I knew I'd never been. For some reason, I filled with shame. He asked about my family.

"You have to honor your parents."

"Honor your parents?" What an old-fashioned expression.

I looked all around at the people in the restaurant. I'd never seen Jews like these before. The women wore long sleeves and long dresses. It was strange. It bothered me.

He tipped his head toward the two girls sitting at the counter to our left and said, "They are Orthodox." He asked some more questions, then took out a pen. On the back of the restaurant bill, he started writing something. He was leaning over the table, scrunched up in intense concentration, mouthing something to himself, erasing, rewriting. Ten minutes or so later he handed me the paper on which he had written, with the childlike, scrawled awkwardness that made it obvious the English alphabet was not his own, a list of some sort of sentences, in carefully executed capital letters. The first one went as follows:

"BARUCH ATAH HASHEM, ELOKEINU MELECH HAOLAM, BOREI MINEI MEZONOT."

He explained that these were blessings in Hebrew to be made over various foods, and told me what kind of food each one was for.

He told me how to light two candles every Friday night for Shabbos. I'd always liked candles. I was surprised we Jews did something so aesthetically appealing. What was Shabbos? He said that's how Jews celebrate the creation of the world every week. What a beautiful idea—I'd never heard such a thing. He told me I should continue living with my parents, and to work for my father in his office.

He wrote down his name. I saw that he was a rabbi. "Call me if you need help!"

He motioned to the waitress and in another language—Hebrew, I gathered—ordered something else. She returned with what I would learn later was poppy-seed cake.

"Don't be scared," he said. "Say this." He pointed to the first line. I read it out loud, and was about to say something when he pressed a finger to his lips. "*Ssshhhh!* Eat!"

It was good.

A few years later, in my first week in Israel, a rabbi at the table spoke about the *parshah*. There was a donkey, he said, whose eyes were opened by Hashem. She saw an angel and at first couldn't speak. *That was me*, I thought.

I felt at home in Jerusalem, so I stayed, and married, and

Hashem gave children, and grandchildren. But from that first Shabbos on, through all the unceasing changes that were to come, one of the things that endured for me was *Balak*. It drew me inexplicably, and spoke for me. It was the *parshah* I always loved most and looked forward to, increasingly, year by year.

One day a quarter-century after my *aliyah*, a friend showed me a program on her computer that computed Gregorian and Hebrew dates. I wanted to know the *parshah* of my Bas Mitzvah. I typed in my birth date, pressed a few keys, and …

"Don't tell me …," said my bus-mate Batsheva.

"Yes. *Balak*."

"Hmm. You know, there's one *parshah* I was always drawn to, too. *Vayera*. I wonder …? It's the one I've always especially liked teaching. Maybe I'll ask my husband to check."

The phone was ringing when I got home. It was Batsheva saying, "You're not going to believe this."

A REFORM *Jew from* ELKINS PARK

BY SUSAN ROSENBERG

S ixty-four years ago, my husband's rabbi changed my whole attitude toward being Jewish, and even today I think of his sermon when I say the Aleinu. I was raised in a Reform home by parents who took great pride in their ignorance of Judaism. "Just be a good American," my father told me, "and that's being a good Jew." After I graduated high school, I met a University of Pennsylvania student from Cleveland. Unlike me, he came from a more traditional, Conservative Jewish home.

How did we meet? Well, it was wartime. He had been commissioned as an officer in the U.S. Navy, and despite our parents' protests that we were too young, that it was wartime and not a time to be married, that it was important for me to finish my education, and so on, we still wanted to get married. Dick was to be sent to a special communications school in Portland, Maine, for six weeks (which seemed like a lifetime to us then), so we were able to persuade our parents to let us marry.

After the war my husband took me to his synagogue so he could thank Hashem for saving his life. There I listened to the rabbi saying that the majority of Jews in the world were proud of being Jewish, wanted to maintain their identity as Jews and thanked Hashem every day for not making them like other peoples of the earth. What? What was that? Those astounding words were so opposite to the attitudes I had formed during my self-hating upbringing. I, who had always been ashamed of being Jewish, who had wanted to blend into the mainstream and hide my identity, was shocked to hear the rabbi speaking of our people with such pride. It was not in the sense of vanity that he used the word "pride," but in the sense of self-esteem. He said that we Jews believe we are required to carry out an important mission in the world. He spoke earnestly and he believed that as an American, his rights to his convictions were guaranteed. He made a virtue of being different. He pointed out that it takes great courage to be different.

Listening, I realized that there were many other ways of looking at things that had never before occurred to me. All the Jews I had ever known saw things from pretty much the same vantage point as I did. Of course, I had recently become aware that my husband and his family thought otherwise, but I believed they were exceptions to the rule, rather unique oddities. Now I was being told that their ideas were similar to those held by the majority of Jews.

It was as if my entire world had been turned upside down. The thought that there were so many Jews who were actually different out of choice, because they wanted to be and not just because it was an unfortunate accident of birth, came as a revelation to me. Certainly, I considered, it is better to be proud of being Jewish than it is to be ashamed. I decided then and there that I wanted our children to grow up with Jewish pride, as I stood and read the translated words of *Aleinu*:

"It is our duty to praise the Master of all, to ascribe greatness to the Molder of primeval creation, for He has not made us like the nations of the lands and has not placed us like the families of the earth; for He has not assigned our portion like theirs nor our lot like all their multitudes ...."

The prayer took on great meaning and has, even after all these years, remained a reminder to me of that time when I first had a change of heart.

There was another reason for wanting to raise our children as Jews. I could visualize Jewish tradition as a long, long chain reaching back from my husband, to his parents, grandparents, and great-grandparents, far back into an invisible past. Though my own family had cast it aside and though I did not yet understand its value, I did understand how precious it was to my husband and to his dear ones. I did not want to be responsible for ending that chain. If I could help it, I vowed to myself, our children would not be missing links.

In 1975, after my mother-in-law, *z"l*, died, my husband began going to the Orthodox *shul* in our neighborhood to say Kaddish. On Saturdays, I also attended and was received with such warmth and generosity of spirit by the women of the congregation that I did not mind sitting behind the *mechitzah*. They helped me follow the prayers without an English translation, and today, *baruch Hashem*, I too am a part of the congregation. My husband still attends *shul* every morning, and we have been blessed with many children, grandchildren and great-grandchildren.

When we are with them in the synagogue or together around the Shabbos table in our home or in theirs, and when we celebrate the holidays together, it is with understanding and meaning. When I see our younger great-grandchildren participating in prayer, I am so very grateful to Hashem who has sustained us and enabled us to reach this season together. I have kept the promise I made to myself. We observe Jewish law and believe in Judaism and in the destiny of our people. All the same, every once in a while I make a mistake (or don't know) about a small prohibition, and my husband lovingly teases me with, "Well, what can you expect? That's what you get when you marry a Reform Jew from Elkins Park."

CALLING OUT *from* *the* DEPTHS

BY SUSAN SCHWARTZ

*T*here is a prayer attributed to the Chazon Ish that was printed on a sticky label to insert in a *siddur,* and given to me many years ago by a friend. Loosely translated it says, "Hashem, please let my children be raised to follow in the ways of Your Torah, show them mercy and turn them away from the temptations that may keep them from following in those ways."

Every morning when I would recite this prayer, I would picture my three boys. The oldest, although a yeshiva graduate and observant of the *mitzvos,* always seemed to me to need strengthening in this department. The middle son seemed strong, but one can never be too sure in today's world with all its competing forces. The youngest was just starting out and certainly could use all the help he could get.

The years went by and I continued to faithfully say this prayer, hoping that my words were being heard and answered. My oldest son was successful in the business world, but I continued to be concerned about what I perceived as a lack of inner spiritual strength.

The letter was the third one we received from our oldest son. Married for eight years, his life seemed to seesaw between happiness and despair. As parents, we prayed for their *shalom bayis* and watched from afar as life spiraled downward for him and his family. The divorce seemed inevitable, and we were grateful for his many friends who were so supportive at a difficult time. As often happens when people hit rock bottom, they turn to Hashem in a final understanding that this is what they were lacking all along, and perhaps this lack contributed to their downfall.

I read the letter with tears in my eyes:

"My learning is going quite well. I am about twenty *blatt* into *Yoma* and I am learning Daf Yomi and keeping up-to-date. We are about fifteen *blatt* into *Kesubos* and I hope by Chanukah to be done with the *mishnayos* of *Seder Moed*. I also started learning *Daniel* with someone here. I am going to try to keep a *seder* in *Navi* as well. I really need to figure out a plan for *chazarah*. I review the *perek* of *mishnayos* I did the day before, every day. So at least I am doing a little bit. But I really need to figure out a longer term plan."

It was a beautiful letter. I was actually very proud of this young man who, once post-high school yeshiva was over, rarely opened a *sefer*, and certainly did not devote time each day to learning.

The letter was written from Federal prison.

Many people find it strange that I can smile when I talk about my son who today sits in prison for committing a white-collar crime that he foolishly thought would solve all his problems. But I am able to recognize Hashem's hand, for without this terrible event, I do not know what would have become of my son. Today he sits and learns and has made Hashem an integral part of his life.

Hashem really does know how to answer a mother's prayers, albeit in a way that we mortals do not always understand. What could have been a time of total demoralization and despair turned into a time of "turning away from temptations and turning to Torah." My son has five *sedarim* a day, is the *gabbai* in his community and has found his way.

And each day when I say the prayer of the Chazon Ish, I still think of my three sons. And I thank Hashem each day for answering a mother's prayers.

To write to Jewish prisoners in prison contact:

Ralph & Pat Holmes
Pen Pal Coordinators
THE ALEPH INSTITUTE
coordinator@jewishpenpals.org
www.jewishpenpals.org

OUT OF THIS WORLD

THE BLESSING *of* CLOSURE

BY SHAYNA HUNT

I suppose it would be easier to simply say that all our relationship issues stemmed from the fact that I had started to become *frum* at the age of sixteen. However, that wouldn't be altogether true. Suffice it to say, a relationship with my mother was never easy to cultivate. Even so, somewhere in the mix of our virulent relationship there were beautiful pockets of tender affection of love. Nevertheless, finding them was always the trick, and as the years went on, they became harder and harder to find.

About a year and a half ago, my husband and I made our usual appointment with Rav David Hanania Pinto of France. He visits Chicago about once a year and meets with people and gives them *brachot*. In the last four years, we hadn't missed one appointment to see him. The meeting usually lasts several minutes, and we always leave with a good feeling. On that particular visit, it began as usual. We gave the *Rav* our Hebrew names, and the names of our children, and waited for the usual *brachah* so we could be on our way.

"Have you seen your mother recently?" the *Rav* asked me, and I nearly fell off my chair. My heart began to pound, and I heard the blood rushing in my ears. The *Rav* repeated his question to me.

"I … that is … I mean … no, actually, I haven't. It's a long story, but we haven't spoken in a long time now. It's very complicated," I barely managed to explain, feeling that old familiar shame of having a dysfunctional relationship with my mother.

The *Rav* directed his pure eyes into mine and very carefully slowly stated, "You need to go see her!" I was dumbfounded. I never mentioned my rocky relationship with my mother, or that I hadn't seen her in a few years.

"I don't think I can. I mean, she won't see me. I've tried before to make peace, but she's an angry person and she won't see me," I tried to explain, hoping he'd understand a situation even I barely knew how to describe.

"She's very sick. And you need to go see her," was all he said.

"What if she won't agree to see me?" I asked fearing rejection, fearing a fight, fearing the fact that I might open a can of worms I would never be able to close again!

"Go see her!" The *Rav* exclaimed, and then gave us our *brachot*. The discussion about my mother was over.

I was an emotional mess for the next few days. About four days after seeing Rav Pinto, I made an appointment to see my own *Rav* regarding all this. I explained the situation and further explained how no one in my family spoke to my mother any more because she suffered from a severe anger and relationship issue. My *Rav* was kind and listened to my reasons and fears about seeing my mother, or even just calling her up. I detailed to him my previous attempts and the toxic outcome they had produced. He personally felt that regardless of the emotional duress I might suffer by contacting my mother, the *shailah* wasn't his to fully answer. He suggested I write to Rav Pinto and explain in detail my reasons for not wanting to start something with my mother that in the end I might not be able to handle. So I did.

Rav Pinto's response was simple and kind. He agreed that I should only do what I felt I could do, and he added that he would give me another *brachah* that things should work out. When I read his letter back to me, I felt immense relief. I was off the hook. I didn't feel obliged to contact my mother. That was at the end of November 2004.

However, over those next few weeks, my mind kept replaying over and over what the *Rav* had initially told me about my mother being sick. My fear was overshadowed by the regret I would feel if, in fact, what the *Rav* had said was true and I had done nothing. Spiritually, something inside me shifted. My fear was somehow less overwhelming, and I made plans to contact my mother. On December 29, her birthday, I arranged to have flowers delivered, and a few days before, I sent a card and pictures of my children through the mail, which would arrive on her birthday. That day I was more nervous than I had been in a long while. Each time the phone rang, I jumped. Had she gotten them yet? Was she angry? Would she be nice?

By dinner time that night she called. I answered the phone and she was cordial, not necessarily nice, but she thanked me for the flowers and asked to speak with my children. Before I passed the phone over to them, I asked after her health. She was vague but said she hadn't been feeling well. I asked if it was serious, but she didn't answer me one way or the other. She didn't want to discuss it with me.

After that day, I continued to send her cards asking if we could come to see her. She called once and asked me to stop sending her things and said that she didn't want to see me. Her anger was back. Nonetheless, I continued to send her pictures and cards. The following fall, my husband and I went back to see Rav Pinto. We received our *brachah,* but there was no mention of my mother.

That December, like the previous one, I sent flowers and a picture gift. My mother was enraged and out of control. Her manic issue was full force, and what I had feared was happening. A week after things cooled down, I made a decision. I davened to Hashem to help soften her heart; I could do no more for my part. The rejection left such a bad taste in my mouth that I found myself thinking of her more than usual and longing for something that I had never had with her.

Then Erev Pesach of this year (2006), out of the blue, I received a note in the mail from my mother. It was surprisingly simple and devoid of anger. She wanted to see us … me and my husband and our children. I was scared but happy. I wrote her back and gave her some dates when we would be available to go to her house. She wrote back the date that was good for her and offered to pay for lunch if we picked it up from somewhere kosher before we drove out to her house. I was impressed with her consideration and her willingness to have us over.

Pesach came and went, and our lunch date was soon approaching. Then I got a call from my aunt. She hadn't talked to my mother in a while as well, but my mother called her to call me and let me know our lunch date would have to be postponed because my mother was in the hospital with a kidney infection. It didn't seem life-threatening at all, but she was unsure of when she'd be going home. My oldest daughter called my mother and they spoke for a little while. My mother didn't feel up to speaking with me. I kept up with the situation through my aunt. Apparently, my mother was released to go home but was right back in the hospital three days later. It was around then that my mother called me and left a message on my answering machine. I called her that night. We spoke for nearly four hours. When she directed the conversation into an area that I knew would end in a fight, I tried a new approach. I told her how much I honestly enjoyed speaking with her and that I enjoyed when we got along.

"Let's avoid topics that get you angry," I told her. "I don't want to make you mad. I like being your friend!" She replied she did, too, and I sensed her vulnerability.

My mother's health continued to decline. The doctors were not sure what was wrong with her and at first they suspected something serious like leukemia. I kept asking her to let me come to see her, but she would get angry and tell me she didn't look good and refused to let me come and see her like that. So we began to speak with each other on the phone several times a day. When the doctors ruled out leukemia, I began to get suspicious of her medical care. She was clearly getting sicker. When I questioned it, she remained steadfast and independent, and I was informed that at sixty-five years old she could "take care of myself, thank you very much!"

A week later, my mother informed me that they believed her illness to be psychosomatic. My aunt called me and was confused at the turn of events. My mother herself was unwilling to really talk about it, and compounded with all the other emotional issues she already had, I could tell she was slipping into a depression. I felt the icy fingers of fear clutch at my heart.

I replayed Rav Pinto words to me from over a year and a half ago, "She's very sick. And you need to go see her!"

That afternoon, regardless of my mother's protests, my husband and I drove an hour and a half to the hospital. From that point on, I informed my mother, the nurses and all her doctors that I was taking charge of my mother's care. I was overwhelmed by my mother's willingness to relinquish control of her care to me. She went as far as requesting to see her lawyer to legally give me power of attorney. From that point on, every hour in my day was spent on my mother ... from making sure she was well taken care of, to fighting the doctors to test her further to find out what was wrong with her. I insisted she was sick, and I demanded that they get to the bottom of it and not simply blame all her symptoms on her emotional issues.

They did find out what was wrong with her, and regretfully,

it was too far gone to treat. She was diagnosed with aggressive liver and lung cancer in the middle of June. For the next three weeks, I barely did anything else but take care of my mother. I moved her to a kosher nursing facility closer to my home. I spent my days settling her affairs according to her wishes and spent quality time with her. At the end, there was nothing left between us but that precious love that had always been so hard to come by. We talked a lot; not a moment we spent together was wasted. We declared our love to each other over and over, both verbally and physically. I relished each bonding hug and each sweet kiss we exchanged. I said things to my mother I had always wanted to say, and she in turn gave to me emotionally all I had ever needed and wanted to hear from her for all the thirty-seven years of my life! I regret nothing except not having her like that with me for longer.

The night before my mother passed away, I had come to her room in the nursing facility around dinner time. I had been there earlier, and she had been in a lot of pain but had been alert. When I walked in that evening, I remember feeling something different in the room. There was a charge of energy all around, and regardless of how strange this sounds, I actually felt my father, *a"h*, and my grandparents, *a"h*, energetically in the room as well. As I made my way to my mother from the doorway, I felt as if unseen energies were parting to let me through. I took one look at my mother and began to cry. I knew that she wasn't long for this world. She was leaving me soon, and I was sad.

I took a chair and pulled it close to her, and as I picked up her cold hand, I told her I was there. I kept telling her how much I loved her and that I was right there with her. Even though she looked like she was sleeping, I could tell she was somewhat alert. I asked her if she was afraid of dying.

"No!" she barked out. "Are you?"

"Am I afraid of you dying?" I clarified.

"Yes!" she replied, the pain in her voice evident.

I began to cry, sobbing so much I could barely answer her clearly for a few minutes. "Yes, I'm afraid to let you go," I managed to say while the tears poured down my cheeks.

"Don't hurt for me!" she said firmly, bravely.

"Okay, I'll try not to," I told her, knowing that I would anyway.

I kissed her soft cheek and continued to hold her hand for a while. A child survivor of the Holocaust, my mother lived her life angry at everyone—but especially at Hashem. I was afraid for her. She never studied the beauty of Torah; she didn't know the meaning of her birthright and the peace it would have offered her at this time—the end of her life. As her only Torah-observant relative, I suppose I felt a protective duty to share with her and help her over to the other side. I began to speak without clearly thinking through my thoughts. They tumbled out, straight from Hashem, and out my mouth.

"Ma," I began, "when you leave your body, don't get confused. Don't stop to think about the fact that you died. Don't look back. Go straight to the Almighty. See the light and just run toward it. Dad will be there and your parents will be there too! And all anyone has left for you is love, pure beautiful love. You just go. Follow Dad and he'll take you where you need to go."

"I will!" she promised me. "He's here now," she ended.

My heart skipped a beat. "Dad? Dad is here?"

"Yes, he's here now," she said, explaining what I had felt when I walked in earlier.

Taking her lead I added, "And your parents are here now, too. There is so much love here for you. They are all here for you."

"Yes," she agreed as she fell asleep.

She slept for about ten minutes, and it was quiet and peaceful in the room. I was silent as I held her hand and stroked her arm with my other hand. Soundless tears would drop occasionally down my cheeks, and I tasted their grief-filled saltiness on my lips. I closed my eyes, and in my mind I saw my dad and my grandparents at the foot of her bed.

Pulled violently out of my peaceful meditation, my mother screamed with an unbelievable strength. "NOW!" she yelled. "SAY IT NOW! AIM—EEEE!" she yelled my English name. "SAY THE JEWISH PRAYER! RIGHT NOW!" the urgency and panic in her demand paralyzed me. I couldn't move, I couldn't speak. Her hand gripped mine hard, and she yelled again.

"SAY THE JEWISH PRAYER NOW!"

And then I did. "*Shema Yisrael*," I began, my body shaking.

With wonder I listened as she fervently repeated each word after me with such a powerful voice. This from a woman who lived her life scoffing at prayers and religion.

"... ECHAD!" she yelled at the end of the first recitation. "AGAIN!" she demanded, and again I complied. She repeated it and yelled "AGAIN" after I finished. Five times over and over we repeated this spiritual dance of prayer. On the fifth time, she fell asleep as her mouth uttered "*Echad*." She slept quietly after that for another ten minutes.

Then she awoke, and with her eyes closed, she called out over my shoulder, "Ma? Ma?" she called to her mother. I answered her in Yiddish, her native language, and speaking as if I was her mother, I told her I was there with her.

"Oh, Ma!" she sighed, relieved, and fell back asleep. I held her hand for another hour or more, and then realizing it was late and she would most likely continue sleeping, I left, planning to come back the next morning.

That night I came home and e-mailed Rav Pinto a letter.

To Rav Pinto—

About a year and a half ago my husband and I met with the Rav in Chicago for a brachah. The Rav mentioned my mother and asked when I had seen her last. I explained briefly how, because of certain issues my mother suffers from, we had not been in contact for a long while. The Rav explained how important it was for me to go see my mother.

Though it was one of the hardest things for me to do, I began to contact my mother several weeks after meeting with the Rav. My mother remained resistant to a meeting. However, I continued to periodically send her things in the mail. Finally, about three months or so ago, my mother finally agreed to see me, my husband and our children. However, several days before our scheduled meeting, I was informed by an aunt that my mother was in the hospital.

My mother has yet to come out of the hospital. She was misdiagnosed continually, until finally, three weeks ago, she was informed that she had untreatable, aggressive cancer of the liver and lung. Each day she slips farther and farther away.

However, amidst the deep regret and sadness of this situation lies the true brachah that both my mother and I have been honored with. Because of my mother's issues, she has driven most of her family and friends away. Holding on to the precious words the Rav said to me when I received my brachah, I pushed through my mother's hard exterior, and I have been with her every day through this horrible experience. She was no longer able to care for herself, and I alone have centered my life around hers and have taken full legal action to be the one to take care of her. Through doing all of this, somehow my mother has been able to see past her issues for stretches at a time to offer me true love from her heart. That is all I ever wanted from my mother. And it's a miracle to be a recipient of it now.

From this I have learned the true meaning of forgiveness and have embraced it fully; I have no doubt that the Rav petitioned the

Almighty on my behalf and on my mother's behalf. My mother is so ill now that she has mostly stopped talking in the last few days; however, before, when she was talking, she kept telling me that it was a real miracle from Hashem that we reconnected to each other before she got so very sick. My mother did not know I had received a brachah a year and a half earlier, but knows nonetheless that Hashem's hand truly repaired this relationship enough to find healing and closure. On behalf of my mother and myself, I would like to sincerely thank the esteemed Rav for his part in our own personal miracle.

Most sincerely,
Shayna Hunt

The next day, as I was getting ready to go see my mother, she slipped from this world—no doubt into the love that I had promised her. We had become so connected that I knew the instant she left, because an overwhelming sadness came over me as I got ready that morning, and I wondered to myself at that moment if she had died. The phone rang minutes later, confirming the news.

The weeks leading up to her death and the weeks since have been overwhelmingly hard, but they have only served to enrich my life. I had been given the beautiful and precious gift of closure, along with a renewed faith in Hashem, from the magical power of the miracle He bestowed upon my relationship with my mother.

I feel her now sometimes during the day—a fleeting emotion—like the gentle caress of butterfly wings. I savor these feelings because they are beautiful pockets of tender affection from her—of love!

About the AUTHORS

*L*eah Abramowitz is a medical social worker, a writer and a resident of the Jewish Quarter. For the past thirty-five years, she's been co-chairman of *Nefesh Israel* and one of the founders of *Melabev*, the prize-winning organization for the elderly who suffer from Alzheimer's. For the latter contribution, she was recently awarded the Yakir Yerushalayim Award. She authored *Tales of Nehama*. However, her most important role is as a mother and grandmother of a large and growing family.

*O*rly Aish lives in Tel Aviv, where she grew up and raised her three children. She is a former teacher and translator of documentaries and recently very active in community work. She writes short stories. The memorial story that she wrote for her aunt, who perished in the Holocaust as a young child, is being kept in Yad Vashem for posterity.

*A*rlene E. Alyehs was born in the Bronx in the baby boom era and moved to Philadelphia at age seven. She was raised in the suburbs. Her natural Jewish instincts were finally addressed by a young Lubavitcher woman who got her started on her path to *teshuvah* and *aliyah*.

Ms. Alyehs has degrees in English literature and clinical social work, but is most proud of her status as the mother of a *rebbetzin* and bubbie to three, of course, beautiful and brilliant Jewish grandchildren. She lives in Jerusalem, Israel, where she patiently awaits the return of her daughter, son-in-law and the three little ones from *shlichut* in Melbourne, Australia.

*A*dam Berkowitz grew up in the "wilds" of suburban New Jersey, dropping out of Rutgers in his senior year. He chose a cooking career over unemployment and moved to New York to apprentice in the most exclusive French restaurants. Through a misunderstanding, he ended up on a religious kibbutz, where he traded in his chef's hat for gum boots and spent five years acting as a surrogate mother for Sabra calves. He trained in the IDF as a combat medic. After five years he left the kibbutz, firmly committed to leaving religion behind. That decision led him straight to yeshiva in Bat Ayin. Conflicting bus schedules have made it impossible for him to leave. He is married to a wonderful woman and has three *frum*-from-birth Israeli children.

*D*anny Brothers was born and raised in Elkton, Virginia, a small rural town in the Shenandoah Valley. At the College of William and Mary, Danny studied classical civilizations and government, graduating in 2007 with a B.A. in government. During university, he became a *ba'al teshuvah*. In September 2007, he made *aliyah* and currently resides in Jerusalem. By the end of 2008, he will be inducted into the Israeli Army, where he is going to serve in a combat unit.

*C*havi Chamish (nee Sekel) was born in Sydney, Australia. As the youngest child of parents who escaped days before Hitler entered Poland, she spent much of her childhood listening to stories of a vanished era. Chavi received a degree in social work from the University of Sydney. She moved to Israel in 1982. Today, she is a mother and English teacher. In 2005, following a casual conversation with her good friend and writer, Ellen Greenfield, she began recording her stories, a number of which have appeared in *Hamodia* as well as other publications.

*S*hifra Cohen is a pen name.

*Y*ossi Faybish was born and spent his childhood in Romania. He finished his academic studies in Israel, choosing the path of engineering rather than arts, though he has been writing poetry and short stories most of his life. Presently, he lives in Belgium, working in the high-tech industry, yet writing more than ever. He has published one book of memoirs and two poetry books, won an international contest and had some of his poems published in poetry anthologies.

*B*racha Goetz graduated from Harvard University, attended the Medical College of Virginia and went on to study at Ohr Somayach Women's Division in Jerusalem. She is the author of eight children's books, including *The Happiness Box*, *The Invisible Book* and the *What Do You See?* series. Mrs. Goetz is also an editor of books for women, a frequently published poet and the Mentoring Coordinator of the Jewish Big Brother and Big Sister Program in Baltimore.

*P*amela Goldstein, a retired nurse and mother of three, is producer/host of the *Boker Tov* radio show, heard weekly in the Windsor/Detroit area and worldwide on the Internet. She's had several short stories published and has written articles for the Canadian Jewish Congress.

*M*ichelle Gordon is a mother of two grown children and a *savta* of two *sabras*. She lives in Chevy Chase, Maryland, with her husband. In between her frequent trips to Israel, she finds time to pursue her vocation as a physical therapist and her avocation as a freelance writer. She was the winner of the 2007 Yom Yerushalayim Essay Contest sponsored by the OU with her essay, "Jerusalem: A Love Story." She's also had ten essays published in the *Washington Jewish Week.*

*J*on Green (Rabbi Yehiel Grenimann) was born in Australia and lives in Israel. His father, Dov Beryl Grenimann, *z"l,* of Disna, near Vilna, was known in the partisan years as "Boris." He worked as a watchmaker until the age of ninety-five in Melbourne, Australia. He and Jon's late uncle, Fima, were the only two of nine children of Rabbi Yehiel and Shula Grenimann of Disna to survive the Holocaust. They survived by hiding in the Naroch forest from where they fought the Germans for almost four years (1941-44) in the partisan unit of Col. Fyodor Markov. Jon's grandfather, after whom he is named, was a well-known rabbi whose *yichus* derives from the Gaon of Vilna.

*J*udy Gruenfeld was born in Brooklyn, New York, to non-religious parents and moved to New Jersey when she married. She has two sons, one of whom is thirty-nine years old and is autistic. She says she always felt there was a hole in her soul, but when she discovered Yiddishkeit, not only was that hole filled but she had a totally different outlook regarding her special son. He has opened up many doors that otherwise she would not have been privileged to pass through. Judy has been published in several Jewish newspapers and magazines and will be included in another anthology, soon to be released.

*S*ara Debbie Gutfreund received her B.A. from the University of Pennsylvania and her M.A. in family therapy from the University of North Texas. She is currently a writer and psychologist who lives with her husband and children in Telzstone, Israel.

*S*hayna Hunt has been a charismatic storyteller since she first started speaking, but she began to professionally publish her writing ten years ago in both Jewish and secular venues. She lives with her husband and three daughters in Chicago. She loves hearing from readers and can be reached at Shaynamy@aol.com.

*E*llen W. Kaplan is Professor of Theater at Smith College, a Fulbright Scholar (Costa Rica, Hong Kong), and an actor, director and writer. Her plays have been produced in the United States and at the Jewish State Theater in Romania. Ellen has published books and scholarly essays; her recent work also appears in *Our Lives: Anthology of Jewish Women's Writing* and *The Deronda Review*; her poetry has twice won awards in Massachusetts. She teaches theater and writing to women in prison, adult learners, special education students and adjudicated teens.

*R*abbi Zvi Konikov received his rabbinical ordination at the Central Lubavitch Yeshiva in Brooklyn, New York, after completing a two-year rabbinical internship at the Yeshiva Gedola in Johannesburg, South Africa. In 1989, after continuing his studies at the Kollel Menachem of Brooklyn, the Lubavitcher Rebbe, *zt"l*, sent him and his wife as his *shluchim* (emissaries) to Greater Melbourne, Florida. Rabbi Konikov lives in Satellite Beach, Florida, and serves as the spiritual leader and executive director of the Space & Treasure Coasts, Florida Chabad Lubavitch branch. He and his *rebbetzin* Shulamit are the proud parents of nine children, *ka"h*.

*M*ary Kropman was born in Eastern Cape South Africa in 1937. She obtained her social work degree in 1956 at University of Cape Town. She married Robert Kropman in 1958 and has three daughters and thirteen grandchildren. In 1977, she earned an M.A. in applied sociology from UCT. She is now involved as a researcher for Friends of Bet Hatefusoth, South Africa, which has published three volumes on Jewish life in the country communities of South Africa, and she is now busy with volumes four and five.

*R*achel Levine was born in New York to Holocaust survivors. She made *aliyah* to Israel in 1969 together with her family, and attended Michlalah in Bayit Vegan. Today, she is married and is a busy mother and grandmother. Her youngest daughter, born with Down Syndrome, is in the fifth grade in a special education school in Jerusalem.

*D*evorah Lifshutz is a pen name.

*T*ova Rhoem lives in Monsey, New York. She attended Bais Yaakov of Monsey and Me'ohr Seminary. Tova Rhoem is a pseudonym.

*S*ara Yoheved Rigler is the author of the bestseller *Holy Woman* and *Lights from Jerusalem*. She is one of the most popular authors on Aish.com. She is also an international lecturer on the subject of Jewish spirituality and inner growth.

*J*oyce Roseman was born in South Wales, United Kingdom. She studied art in Cardiff before being conscripted for war work during World War II. She was active in various branches of the fashion trade. Joyce came to Israel with her family in 1980. She lives in Petach Tikvah.

*S*usan Rosenberg was born in Atlantic City, New Jersey, in 1924 and grew up in Elkins Park, Pennsylvania, a suburb of Philadelphia. Though her parents belonged to a Reform synagogue, they never attended. Susan grew up religiously deprived and is currently writing a book that attempts to trace her step-by-step progress toward the understanding and practice of Judaism. Susan lived in Haifa from 1949 to 1956 during which time her husband served first as communications officer for the Israeli Navy (*Chayl Hayam*) and then as comptroller for the Alliance Tire Company in Hadera. They went back to the States in 1956 and returned to live in Israel permanently as citizens in 1973.

*R*abbi Yaakov Salomon, C.S.W., is a noted psychotherapist, in private practice in Brooklyn, New York, for over twenty-five years. He is a senior lecturer and the creative director of Aish HaTorah's Discovery Productions. He is also an editor and author for the ArtScroll Publishing Series and a member of the Kollel of Yeshiva Torah Vodaath. Rabbi Salomon is co-author, with Rabbi Noah Weinberg, of the best-selling book *What the Angel Taught You: Seven Keys to Life Fulfillment* and co-producer of the highly acclaimed films, *Inspired, Inspired Too* and *Kiruv Across America*. His most recent book is *Something to Think About: Extraordinary Reflections About Ordinary Events*. Rabbi Salomon is also a featured writer on Aish.com, and writes and produces a weekly video blog, *Salomon Says,* for the site. Rabbi Salomon shares his life with his wife, Temmy, and their unpredictable family.

*M*anuel Sand was born in Romania and immigrated to Canada with his parents when only six months old. He studied at Sir George Williams University, after graduating Baron Byng High School and the Lubavitcher Yeshiva. He married Esther

Ella Bromberg in 1957 and came on *aliyah* to Israel in 1968. He entered the life insurance business in 1963, and was consistently one of the company's top salesmen. He is a life member of M.D.R.T. (Million Dollar Round Table). In Israel, he set up and managed a life insurance company until his retirement in 1987. A devoted family man, he heads the family clan, which today numbers more than forty, *ken yirbu*. All family members live in Israel.

*S*usan **Schwartz** is a wife, mother and grandmother. She has an M.A. degree in social work and resides in Chicago, Illinois. Her work has appeared on Aish.com, and in *Binah Magazine* and other Jewish publications.

*N*achman **Seltzer** is the author of *The Edge, The Link, Nine Out of Ten: The Life Story of Dr. Moshe Katz,* (which was first serialized in *Hamodia,*) *In the Blink of an Eye and Other Stories* and *Stories with a Twist,* a compilation of his short stories. His true-life stories are a frequent addition to the *Hamodia* magazine.

*E*sther **Sender** lives in Jerusalem with her family and writes "Concentric Circles," an inspiring regular column for *Mishpacha Magazine.*

*S*arah **Shapiro** is the author of *Growing with My Children, Don't You Know It's a Perfect World, A Gift Passed Along* and *Wish I Were Here.* She edited the anthology *Of Home and Heart* and the *Our Lives* anthology of Jewish writers, of which volume IV, *All of Our Lives,* is due to be published this year. Her writing has appeared in *The Jewish Observer, The Jewish Week, The Jerusalem Post, International Herald Tribune, Hadassah Magazine, Los Angeles Times, Jewish Action, Binah Magazine,* Aish.com, and other publications. She has served as a columnist for *The New Standard, Hamodia, Mishpacha* and *American Jewish Spirit.* She lives with her family in Jerusalem, and has been giving writing workshops since 1992.

Sheindel Devorah bas Miriam is a pen name.

Miriam Shields is a psychologist who lives in New York. She enjoys creative writing, especially short stories and poetry. Her work has appeared in *Horizons* and on Chabad's website TheJewishWoman.org. She also writes for her husband's health promotion company, *Balanced Living, Inc.*

Sara Layah Shomron made *aliyah* from the United States shortly after graduating from Arizona State University with an M.S. in justice studies. She was twenty-two and a newlywed. She has been privileged to live in the Galilee, Yehuda, Shomron, Gush Katif and presently off the Ashkelon coast. It was in Neve Dekalim, Gush Katif that she, her husband and seven children found their niche. They lived, loved, laughed and thrived in Neve Dekalim for thirteen years until the Israeli unilateral withdrawal and destruction of beautiful Gush Katif. She and her family have taken their positive energy and continue at the Nitzan *caravilla* site, the temporary residence of five hundred Gush Katif families.

Shifra Shomron is a Gush Katif resident-expellee and the teenage author of the historical novel *Grains Of Sand: The Fall Of Neve Dekalim.* She is currently studying to be a high school English and Bible studies teacher in the Israeli government accelerated Excellence B.Ed. Program at Givat Washington College. Visit Shifra's website: www.geocities.com/nevedekalim.

*P*aula R. Steen has been a teacher, school administrator and freelance writer, both in Europe and in the United States. She founded and directs a mentoring program for public school students in Massachusetts, where she also tends her garden.

*M*ikimi Steinberg made *aliyah* in 1979 (her first *Shemittah*) at age sixteen on her own and has lived in the northern part of Eretz Yisrael for most of her life. She has married (and divorced) and also raised a remarkable daughter (now twenty-two years old) in spite of emotional hardships. She has been aided by the ongoing *chessed* of numerous friends in her hometown as well as Jerusalem. She is an aspiring writer with her own unique style to share with the world.

*R*abbi Chaim Steinmetz was born in New York City in 1959. He studied in Telshe Yeshiva in Cleveland, Ohio, under Rabbi Mordechai Gifter, *zt"l*, and considers himself fortunate to be counted among his disciples. Together with Rabbi Sendy Ornstein, he established Renewal in 2006. Having witnessed the pain and suffering of those on dialysis, they felt that something needed to be done to help these people resume living a normal life and restore them to their families. For the past two years, he has been dedicated to developing Renewal, serving as the ultimate resource for those suffering from renal failure, with emphasis on those with ESRD (End-Stage Renal Disease) who are waiting for a transplant. Since 2006, Renewal has, *baruch Hashem,* been involved in thirteen successful transplants.

*S*heindel Weinbach has been translating books for the past three decades. She was a regular columnist for the *Jewish Press* for two decades and family editor for *Yated International,* and is now featured in *Hamodia* in *Lite from Yerushalayim.* As you can see from her story, she is very involved in the *Beged Yad L'Yad* network of used clothing *gemachim* in Israel.

M. **Winner** is a wife and mother living and working in Jerusalem. In addition to constantly striving to outpace her dishes and laundry, she proofreads, edits and writes whenever she can.

*R*abbi Yosef Wolicki is a native of New York. He served as a congregational rabbi in the United States and Canada for twenty-four years. After his *aliyah* in 1986, he joined the faculty of Orot Israel College in Elkana and also worked as a psychologist at Shaare Zedek Hospital, counseling families of patients with Alzheimer's disease. He moved to Netanya in 1990 as the rabbi of the New Synagogue. He retired from the synagogue in 2004 and now lives in Beit Shemesh. He has given seminars in counseling skills and practical rabbinics to young rabbis for the Shaal Program of Yeshivat Shaalvim and is on the faculty of the Israel Center in Jerusalem and Yeshivat Yesodei HaTorah. He leads support groups for families of Alzheimer's sufferers in Beit Shemesh. Rabbi Wolicki and his wife Marsha are the parents of five sons and have twenty-two grandchildren, *ka"h*.

*T*ova Younger, daughter of Holocaust survivors, lived with her husband and children in Los Angeles, California, for over twenty years, working in various positions, including candy distributor, teacher and babysitter, to name a few. To their great joy, their first three children got married and settled in Eretz Yisrael! They decided to join them. There, Tova became a freelance writer, while she and her husband continue raising their family and spending time with her parents who came to Eretz Yisrael a year later.

CREDITS

Some of the stories in this anthology have been previously published in various publications. They are all reprinted with permission.

- ⌘ **"It's Almost Shabbos,"** BY ROSALLY SALTSMAN
  First published in the international *Yated Ne'eman*

- ⌘ **"My JetBlue Minyan,"** BY RABBI ZVI KONIKOV
  First published on www.Chabad.org

- ⌘ **"So What if She's Older than Me?,"** BY RABBI YAAKOV SALOMON
  First published on Aish.com

- ⌘ **"Stones,"** BY CHAVI CHAMISH
  First published in *Hamodia Magazine*

- ⌘ **"The Old Lady,"** BY LEAH ABRAMOWITZ
  First published in *Horizons*

- ⌘ **"From One Second to the Next,"** BY NACHMAN SELTZER
  First published in *Hamodia Magazine*

- ⌘ **"In One Hour,"** BY NACHMAN SELTZER
  First published in *Hamodia*

- ⌘ **"Triumph,"** BY RACHEL LEVINE
  First published in *Horizons*

- ⌘ **"Sweet Nachas,"** BY DEVORAH LIFSHUTZ
  First published in *Binah Magazine* and the international *Yated Ne'eman*

⋗ **"Best Friends,"** by Judy Gruenfeld
A version of this piece appeared in *The American Jewish Times*

⋗ **"Rollercoaster,"** by Sheindel Devorah bas Miriam
First published in the international *Yated Ne'eman*

⋗ **"A Visit from Eliyahu,"** by Rosally Saltsman
First published in the international *Yated Ne'eman*

⋗ **"Coming to America,"** by Miriam Shields
First published in *The Jewish Observer*; also appeared on
www.TheJewishWoman.org

⋗ **"Blessings of the Great-Greats,"** by Michelle Gordon
A version of this piece appeared in *The Washington Jewish Week*

⋗ **"The Velvet Tablecloth,"** by Shayna Hunt
Published in *Horizons* and in *The Jewish Press*

⋗ **"Cookies for Life,"** by Tova Younger
First published in *The Jewish Press* under a pseudonym

⋗ **"Adi's Angel,"** by Sara Yoheved Rigler
First published in *Lights from Jerusalem* (Mesorah
Publications, Ltd.); also appeared on Aish.com

⋗ **"Nachas From the Tzuris,"** by Esther Sender
First published in *Mishpacha Magazine*

⋗ **"To Shake and to be Shaken,"** by Rabbi Yosef Wolicki
First published in *Jewish Spirituality* (The Israel Center,
Jerusalem)

> **"A Donkey in Manhattan,"** BY SARAH SHAPIRO
First published in *Wish I Were Here* (Mesorah Publications, Ltd.)

> **"The Blessing of Closure,"** BY SHAYNA HUNT
First published in *The Jewish Press*; also in *Horizons* (in an abridged form)

> **"What the Taxi Driver Told Us,"** BY SUSAN SCHWARTZ
First published on www.OU.org

All terms are Hebrew unless otherwise specified as Yiddish (Yidd.) or Aramaic (Aram.)

A"h—acronym for "alav/aleha hashalom," may he/she rest in peace

Ad mei'ah v'esrim—until 120

Adar—month in the Jewish calendar (usually coincides with March)

Aleinu—Jewish daily prayer traditionally ascribed to Joshua

Aliyah—immigrating to Israel; being called up to the Torah

Amen—traditional affirmation to a blessing or prayer

Arba Minim—the four species taken on Sukkot

Aufruf (Yidd.)—when a man is called to the Torah, usually on the Sabbath before his wedding in Ashkenazi custom

B'ezras Hashem—with Hashem's help

Ba'al/ba'alat Teshuvah—A man/woman who has become religious

Ba'alei chessed—people who regularly perform acts of kindness

Bachurim—young, unmarried men

Baruch Hashem—thank (lit., "bless") Hashem

Bentched gomel (Yidd.)—recited the blessing of thanksgiving after surviving a dangerous experience

Blatt (Yidd.)—pages of Talmud

Brachah, brachot/s—blessings

Brissen—circumcisions

Brit milah—circumcision

Bubbie/Bubby—grandmother

Bureka—a type of baked or fried filled pastry

Caravilla—a prefabricated home

Chabad — a large Chassidic movement within Orthodox Judaism; "Chabad" is a Hebrew acronym for *Chachmah, Binah*, and *Da'at*, meaning wisdom, understanding, and knowledge

Chabadnikim — members of the Chabad community

Chaggim — holidays

Challah, Challos — special braided loaves of bread used on the Sabbath and holidays

Chareidi — ultra-Orthodox

Chas v'shalom — Heaven forbid

Chassan — groom

Chassidishe — Chassidic

Chatuna/ Chasunah — wedding

Chavrusos — female study partners

Chazarah — review

Cheder — Jewish elementary school

Chessed — kindness

Chizuk — encouragement

Chol Hamoed — The intermediate days of a festival

Chumash/im — the five books of the Torah

Daf Yomi — A special learning program in which the same page of Talmud is learned by participants each day all over the world

Daven (Yidd.) — pray

Dreidel (Yidd.) — spinning top used in a Chanukah game

Dunam — a unit of area used in the Ottoman Empire and still used, in various standardized versions, in many countries formerly part of the Ottoman Empire

Echad — one

Eliyahu Hanavi — Elijah the Prophet

Eretz Yisrael — the Land of Israel

Erev — eve of

Etrog — citron

Ezer k'negdo — wife (lit., "helpmate opposite him")

Frum (Yidd.) — religiously observant

Gabbai—manager of a synagogue

Gan—kindergarten

Gannenet—kindergarten teacher

Gemach—Hebrew acronym for *"gemilus chassadim,"* doing kindness; free loan society, but *gemach*s also exist for numerous goods and services needed in Orthodox communities

Glatt (Yidd.)—colloquially, "impeccably kosher"

Gush Katif—a bloc of seventeen Israeli settlements in the southern Gaza strip. In August 2005, the 8,000 residents of Gush Katif were forcibly evicted from the area and their homes demolished as part of Israel's unilateral disengagement plan.

Hagaddah—guide book and prayer book that sets out the order of the Passover Seder

Hakadosh Baruch Hu—the Holy One, blessed be He

Hakaras hatov—gratitude

Halachically—according to Jewish law

Haman—the evil enemy of the Jews who tried to annihilate the entire Jewish people during the reign of the Persian/Medean king Achashverosh

Hashem—the Almighty

Hashgachah/hashgachah pratit/s—Divine Providence

Havdalah—service performed at the end of the Sabbath to divide between the Sabbath and the weekdays

Ima—mommy

Jid—derogatory word for Jew

Kaddish—prayer that publicly sanctifies the name of Hashem; also know as the mourner's prayer

Kallah—bride

Kashrut—laws of keeping kosher

Kayn ayin hara/ka"h (Yidd.)—without the evil eye

Kever—grave

Kiddush Hashem—Sanctification of Hashem's name

Kippah—skullcap

Klal Yisrael—the Jewish people

Kollel—yeshiva for married men

Korban—sacrifice

Kotel—the Western Wall

Kugel (Yidd.)—a variety of traditional baked Jewish side dishes or desserts

Kvell (Yidd.)—take pride

Lein (Yidd.)—to read publicly from the Torah or other books of Scripture following the traditional cantillation marks

Licht (Yidd.)—light, refers to candles lit at the beginning of the Sabbath or a festival

Litvak (Yidd.)—Lithuanian

Lulav—palm frond

Maggid, maggidim—storyteller(s)

Malina (Yidd.)—hiding place

Mashgiach—spiritual supervisor

Mechilah—forgiveness

Mechitzah—partition separating men and women in a synagogue

Megillah—Book of Esther

Mekubal, mekubalim—a person/people trained in the study of Kabbalah (Jewish mysticism) who are believed to have special spiritual insight

Mikvah—ritual bath

Minyan—quorum of ten men required for public prayer

Mishnayos—sections of Mishnah, the Oral Torah as codified by Rabbi Yehuda Hanasi

Mitzvot, mitzvos—Torah commandments

Mordechai—one of the heroes in the Purim miracle, who led the Jews to repent and thereby helped bring about their salvation

Nachas—pride and joy

Navi—prophet

Neft—kerosene

Neiro ya'ir—may his candle continue to cast light

Neis, nissim — miracle

Neshamah, neshamos — soul(s)

Nifteres — deceased female

Olim — immigrants to Israel

Parnassah — livelihood

Parshah — weekly Torah portion

Parshas — the weekly Torah portion of

Perek — chapter

Pesach — Passover

Pesukim — verses from holy texts

Peyos — sidelocks

Pintele Yid (Yidd.) — spark of a Jewish soul

Potch (Yidd.) — smack

Rabbanim — rabbis

Rachmana litzlan (Aram.) — may Hashem have mercy

Rasha — evil person

Rav — rabbi

Rebbe (Yidd.) — Chassidic rabbi and leader

Rebbetzin (Yidd.) — a rabbi's wife; alternatively, a very learned woman

Rebbi, rebbeim — Torah teacher(s)

Refuah — healing

Roshei yeshiva — heads of yeshivas

Sabba — grandfather

Sabra — native Israeli named after indigenous Israeli cactus

Savta — grandmother

Seder, sedarim — learning period(s)

Sefer Torah — Torah scroll

Seudah — festive meal

Seudas hoda'ah — feast of thanksgiving

Sevivon, sov, sov, sov — Chanukah song about the dreidel game

Shabbasos — Sabbaths

Shabbos — the Sabbath

Shabbosdik (Yidd.) — appropriate for the Sabbath

Shacharit — morning prayers

Shailah—question pertaining to Jewish law

Shalom bayis—peace in the home (usually between husband and wife)

Shema Yisrael—prayer affirming a Jew's faith in Hashem

Shemos—Exodus

Sheva brachos—the week following a wedding, during which every time the newly married couple has a meal with a *minyan* present, seven special blessings are recited; the seven blessings recited during a wedding ceremony

Shidduch—match, date

Shpiel (Yidd.)—humorous play or skit

Shuk—marketplace

Shul—synagogue

Siddur—prayer book

Simchah—joy; a happy event

Sukkah—a temporary dwelling that Jews use during the holiday of Sukkot

Sukkos, Sukkot—holiday that commemorates how Hashem sheltered the Jews during their forty-year stay in the desert

Tanach—the Bible

Tatti (Yidd.)—daddy

Tefillin—phylacteries; a pair of black leather boxes containing scrolls of parchment inscribed with Torah verses, worn by adult Jewish men during morning prayers

Tehillim—Psalms

Teshuvah—repentance

Tikkun—rectification of a past deed

Treif (Yidd.)—unkosher

Tzaddik, tzaddikim—righteous person(s)

Tzenter (Yidd.)—last person needed to complete a *minyan*

Tzioni—Zionist

Tzitzis/tzitzit—ritual fringed garment worn by Jewish males

Tzuris (Yidd.)—troubles

Ulpan—class in which new immigrants to Israel learn Hebrew

Viduy—confessional prayer said on Yom Kippur and on one's deathbed

Yad Hashem—the guiding hand of Hashem

Yerushah—inheritance

Yerushalayim—Jerusalem

Yeshiva, yeshivos—Torah school(s)

Yiddishe (Yidd.)—Jewish

Yiddishkeit (Yidd.)—Judaism

Yom tov—holiday

Z"l—Hebrew acronym for *zichrono/a livrachah*, may his/her memory be for a blessing

Zechus—merit

OTHER BOOKS BY ROSALLY SALTSMAN:

- ⸖ Finding the Right Words
- ⸖ Parenting by the Book
- ⸖ Soul Journey
- ⸖ A Portion of Kindness

MUSIC:

- ⸖ Like a Rose Among the Thorns

ROSALLY'S WEBSITE:

- ⸖ http://www.shemayisrael.com/publicat/rosallysaltsman/